Raves for *Fundraisin* ...

For nonprofit organizations ....omy, *Fundraising When Money Is Tight* presents the road map to survival—and a bright future beyond. Mal Warwick's seasoned judgment can help preserve the vital role of the nonprofit sector in educating our young, feeding the hungry, sheltering the homeless, healing the sick, celebrating our diverse culture, and restoring the environment.

— Congresswoman Barbara Lee, chair, Congressional
Black Caucus

Professionals and volunteers in nonprofits looking for ways to weather this economic storm must digest Mal Warwick's timely book. *Fundraising When Money Is Tight* takes the panic out of today's uncertainty by offering up reasoned strategies to achieve organizational success in a declining economy.

— H. Art Taylor, president and CEO, BBB Giving Alliance

This is a valuable book because it details stuff you can actually do. Mal Warwick has given us a simple outline for making sure we stabilize our existing program, not lose sight of the need to be aggressive at times and cautionary at other times, while laying the groundwork for weathering storms in the future. And unlike many such guidebooks, this stuff can be accomplished by any organization regardless of size, complexity, or sophistication. This is a valuable tool for fundraisers.

— Kurt Aschermann, president, Charity Partners
Foundation, and consultant

As a practitioner, Mal Warwick has spent a lifetime learning and teaching how to fundraise more effectively. His latest book is another in a series of gems, laser-focused to help us succeed—and his experience shines through again in this must-have guide for today's economic climate.

—Dr. Mark S. Albion, former professor of marketing, Harvard Business School, and *New York Times* best-selling author, *Making a Life, Making a Living*

Fundraising When Money Is Tight is the book every fundraising professional needs to read immediately. It's to the point, filled with both the "hard facts" and "realistic steps" that development shops, large and small, must understand and implement now rather than later.

—Judith E. Nichols, author, *Pinpointing Affluence in the 21st Century*

Too many fundraisers will use the recession as an excuse for underperforming when there is actually considerable scope for optimism. Warwick shatters our misconceptions and maps out practical steps that all organizations can take to not only weather the storm but be in better shape because of it.

—Adrian Sargeant, PhD, Robert F. Hartsook Professor of Fundraising, Indiana University–Purdue University Indianapolis

I've been waiting for a book like this. It provides a step-by-step approach to maximize revenue in the current economy and prepare for better times to come. It's filled with hundreds of examples and tips. There are fifteen chapters, and each alone is worth the price of the book.

— Jerold Panas, executive partner, Jerold Panas,
   Linzy & Partners

Fundraising When Money Is Tight is the trifecta: sound philosophy, practical strategies, and hands-on examples. Don't put Mal's guide on your bookshelf. Place it on your desk. Read it. Use it!

— Roger M. Craver, chair, DonorTrends, and editor,
   www.TheAgitator.net

Mal Warwick doesn't sell quick fixes and silver bullets—even in times of trouble. He offers specific, practical steps to cut costs and improve fundraising performance. He demands the best: donor-focused relationship building, strategic thinking, top-notch strategy, and competence. And he rewards us with both the "why" and the "how."

— Simone P. Joyaux, ACFRE, author, *Keep Your Donors*
   and *Strategic Fund Development*

In *Fundraising When Money Is Tight*, Mal Warwick provides solid strategic and tactical insights of how best to lead our organizations during times of uncertainty. I found this book to be not only a quick, interesting read, but also an important guide for making critical decisions today and tomorrow.

— Kory Christianson, CFRE, St. Joseph's Indian School

Take Mal's "exercise in visioning," and use as many as you can of Mal Warwick's dozens of cost-cutting ideas—all to enhance your net revenue today and increase your program's potential for the future.

— James M. Greenfield, ACFRE, FAHP, author,
  *Fundraising Fundamentals: A Guide to Annual
  Giving for Professionals and Volunteers*

Whether you're working at the Board level or looking for specific tactics to get you through challenging times, *Fundraising When Money Is Tight* is a must-read. Full of smart advice and proven approaches that have always made sense, and never more so than now.

— Phyllis Freedman, president, SmartGiving

Fundraising When Money Is Tight is both timely and timeless. Development staff looking for creative ideas and encouragement in dealing with the current economic crisis will find them in this book. But every organization will face other crises. Donors will change priorities, board members will fade away, direct mail and online copy will lose their zing—and this book will come in handy once again. Its checklists, samples, and down-to-earth advice will reassure seasoned professionals that they are on the right track and open new vistas for those on their way up.

— Sandra A. Adams, vice president,
  Grameen Foundation

In this engaging and accessible book, Mal Warwick manages to distill and download over 30 years of social justice activism and professional fundraising expertise. *Fundraising When Money Is Tight* provides us with the tools to continue to dream for a better world.

— Belvie Rooks, board chair, Ella Baker Center for Human Rights, and board member, Jessie Smith Noyes Foundation

I've relied on Mal and his firm since 1997, and his advice has helped build and expand our grassroots operation through the years.

— U.S. Senator Russ Feingold

Tough times or high times, this is a book that every nonprofit should read. The strategies, tips, research, reminders, and challenges have been integrated into a readable, practical, and thoughtful book that will be relevant far longer than the current economic crisis.

— Kay Sprinkel Grace, author, consultant, and principal, Transforming Philanthropy

When Mal Warwick writes a book, you should to read it. Mal's experience and insights are unparalleled. Although this book is written specifically to address the challenging times in which we find ourselves, there are timeless strategies here that will be all the more relevant in the good times that assuredly are ahead.

— Christopher G. Cleghorn, former executive vice president, Easter Seals

In *Fundraising When Money Is Tight*, Mal Warwick has managed to incorporate wise and complex concepts in easy-to-understand—and easy-to-read—language. Right after reading this book, I was able to put his advice to use at a planning session with senior staff and campaign volunteer leadership.

— Roberta Zucker Catalinotto, chief development officer,
Jewish Community Federation of San Francisco,
the Peninsula, Marin & Sonoma Counties

Mal Warwick gives us some very useful suggestions on how we can meet growing need during difficult times. I highly recommend *Fundraising When Money Is Tight*.

— Michael Welch, associate director, Office of Medical
Development, Stanford University

Fundraisers bring passion to work with them every day—that's why they're fundraisers. Mal Warwick has shown us how to take that passion, no matter how challenging the times, and use it in support of the causes that we work for. Mal's new book encourages all of us to recognize that our professional abilities are more relevant when money is tight and helps to provide the focus that we need to maximize our impact on the causes that we work for.

— Andrew Watt, FInstF, chief programs officer, Association
of Fundraising Professionals

Praise from Around the World

You lose the right to complain about this economic downturn if you haven't read and put into practice the tips in Mal Warwick's new book. Regardless of the economy, this short book is a great read and embodies great fundraising practice. An essential read for all fundraisers and those they report to.

— Sean Triner, co-founder, Pareto Fundraising (Australia)

This is a wonderful, helpful book that should be on the must-read list for every board member and every fundraiser. Mal offers a thoughtful, strategic approach that will serve you well—in good times and in bad.

— Harvey McKinnon, author, *The Power of Giving* (Canada)

Fundraisers should work as if money is always tight. That's why I like this book a lot. It's timely, sure, but it's also well-informed, perceptive, practical, and well-written. There are lots of new thoughts and tips, yet much of what Mal sets out is simply good fundraising practice, reworked for now and the foreseeable future.

— Ken Burnett, managing trustee, www.sofii.org, and author, *Relationship Fundraising* (France)

With this great book, Mal Warwick proves that fundraisers should always work on the basis of a solid strategy. Touching on all the important aspects of adapting and maintaining a strategy, enabling long-term growth, and preserving the capacity to resist future crises, Mal shows the way out of this down period—and the way to avoid the next one.

— Jan Krol, co-chair, Resource Alliance (Netherlands)

Worried? I am, too. But after reading Mal Warwick's latest, I have some optimism. We *can* beat this thing.

— Steve Thomas, CFRE, chair, Stephen Thomas Ltd. (Canada)

Some fundraisers are just starting to understand the economic crisis. Mal Warwick has analyzed it systematically. In *Fundraising When Money Is Tight*, he presents specific, concrete recommendations for an approach to fundraising that will be best for your organization no matter how severe conditions become.

— Ole von Uexküll, executive director, Right Livelihood Award Foundation (Sweden)

The advice in this book is plain good common sense—but then the best advice always is.

— Simon Collings, chief executive, Resource Alliance (UK)

When there is danger, some people react like rabbits, sitting in a hole and waiting. Others are like antelopes, running away (and it hardly matters where). This book kindly, simply, and effectively guides both rabbits and antelopes to act rationally to suit the circumstances and win their future.

— Jana Ledvinova, co-chair, Czech Fundraising Center (Czech Republic)

In case of economic crisis, break glass—and read this book. A solid document with a practical guide to survive in a storm.

— Marcelo Iniarra, tribe chief, www.marceloiniarra.com, and former international fundraising and campaign innovation manager, Greenpeace International (Argentina)

I am relieved and empowered by reading *Fundraising When Money Is Tight*. It is not just for people who need a guide to fundraising in an economic crisis. This encouraging book provides a bottom-up approach to fundraising based on personal experience. You will enjoy Mal's humor, insight, and warm heart.

— YoungWoo Choi, president and CEO, Doum & Nanum (South Korea)

Brilliant! If you follow even half the advice Mal lays out so clearly in this book, you'll raise more money and spend less on fundraising costs. As a professor in a post-grad college program in Fundraising and Volunteer Management, I can't think of a better book to explain sophisticated fundraising techniques in simple terms. Bravo!

— Professor Ken Wyman, CFRE, program coordinator,
   Post-Graduate Fundraising and Volunteer Management,
   Humber College (Canada)

Fundraising has always been unpredictable and imprecise — more so in difficult times. Prudence suggests applying the simple, logical, but vigorous steps suggested by Mal Warwick in his new book, *Fundraising When Money Is Tight*. Happy reading and applying! Why am I saying this? I have tried this approach, and it works.

— Maj. Gen. Surat Sandhu (Ret.), chair,
   South Asian Fund Raising Group (India)

Fundraising When Money Is Tight

Fundraising When Money Is Tight

A Strategic and Practical Guide
to Surviving Tough Times
and Thriving in the Future

Mal Warwick

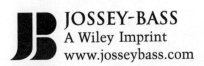

JOSSEY-BASS
A Wiley Imprint
www.josseybass.com

Published by Jossey-Bass
A Wiley Imprint
989 Market Street, San Francisco, CA 94103-1741—www.josseybass.com

Jossey-Bass books and products are available through most bookstores. To contact Jossey-Bass directly call our Customer Care Department within the U.S. at 800-956-7739, outside the U.S. at 317-572-3986, or fax 317-572-4002.

Jossey-Bass also publishes its books in a variety of electronic formats. Some content that appears in print may not be available in electronic books.

Cataloging-in-publication data has been applied for.
ISBN: 978-0-4704-8132-5

Printed in the United States of America
FIRST EDITION
PB Printing   10 9 8 7 6 5 4 3 2 1

CONTENTS

CONTENTS

WHO SHOULD READ THIS BOOK

READ THIS BOOK...

- ... if you're wondering whether economic troubles will induce your donors to simply stop giving and force you to cut your operations to the bone—or worse.
- ... if you're facing a choice between cutting fundraising and marketing costs or laying off program staff.
- ... if you serve in a leadership role in a nonprofit cause, organization, or institution as executive director, development director, controller, financial manager, or marketing director or as a member of the board of trustees.
- ... if you're involved in a fundraising, development, or membership-building program for your organization.
- ... if you contribute money or time to a public interest group or a charity.
- ... if you're involved in public relations or advertising for one or more nonprofit organizations.
- ... if you've taken an interest in the activities of a public interest organization or a charity as a reporter, news producer, consultant, student, or donor.

- ... or if you simply want to understand better how difficult economic times affect the nonprofit sector—and what nonprofit organizations and institutions can do about it.

ACKNOWLEDGMENTS

*F*undraising *When Money Is Tight* took shape in late November and early to mid-December 2008, mostly on long airplane flights and in hotel rooms at such far-flung locations as Seoul, Korea; Mombasa, Kenya; and Washington, D.C., in between consulting and teaching assignments. No doubt my clients and students suffered the results of my preoccupation with this project, and I extend my sincere apologies to all of them.

This book is a much-expanded version of two short papers I coauthored with Dan Doyle, CEO of Mal Warwick Associates and Donordigital, and distributed widely on the Internet, the first in January 2008, the second in November 2008. Those papers, and this book in turn, benefited not just from Dan's ideas but from the contributions of others on the consulting staff of our two companies, especially Peter Schoewe, Suzie McGuire, Mwosi Swenson, and Bill Rehm at Mal Warwick Associates and Nick Allen and Emily Campbell at Donordigital. Later, Brienne Collison gave me invaluable help as well. I'm especially indebted to Peter Schoewe, Bill Rehm, and Nick Allen for their many constructive corrections, additions, and comments.

But that's only the surface reality. More to the point, the staff of these companies—some of whom I've worked with for more than two decades—have informed my thinking since my early days as a fundraiser. Their work for our clients continuously inspires me and is surely reflected in the pages of this book. Equally important have been the ideas and experience I've gained from the hundreds of nonprofits with which I've personally worked over three decades.

I also owe a debt of gratitude to some of the many fundraising professionals outside my firm who ventured into the public to offer their own insights and conclusions about how fundraisers might best respond to difficult economic conditions. Of the many articles and other publications listed in the Reading List at the end of this book, I've gained the most from observations by Robert F. Sharpe Jr. of The Sharpe Group., who has gone out of his way to lend me a hand at critical times in the development of this book; Tom Belford and Roger Craver of *The Agitator*; Melissa Brown and Patrick Rooney of the Center on Philanthropy at Indiana University; and Holly Hall of the *Chronicle of Philanthropy*. My modest efforts on scenario planning have benefited largely from the insight Peter Schwartz shared in his classic book, *The Art of the Long View*.

By no means last, I must mention my editor at Jossey-Bass, Jesse Wiley. From the moment I called him to suggest this book, Jesse has been supportive far beyond what I could have reasonably expected of a busy editor, among whose many and diverse responsibilities my book must be like a fly on the hide of the proverbial elephant.

I would not have been able to write *Fundraising When Money Is Tight* without the help of all these people. But for good or ill, it was I who wrote it, and if you disagree with what I say here, or are disappointed, blame it on me, not them.

ABOUT THE AUTHOR

Mal Warwick has distinguished himself through his contributions to the nonprofit sector as one of the world's leading authors, consultants, and public speakers on direct response marketing and fundraising for nonprofit organizations and as an advocate for socially and environmentally responsible policies and practices in the private sector.

A serial entrepreneur, Mal has been active in promoting social and environmental responsibility in the business community nationwide for two decades. Along with Ben Cohen, cofounder of Ben & Jerry's, and others, he was a cofounder of Business for Social Responsibility and served on its board during its inaugural year, 1992. In 2001, after more than a decade as an active member of Social Venture Network, he was elected to its board and served as chair (2002–2006). He also was a member of the Founding Advisory Board of the Center for Responsible Business at the Haas School of Business at the University of California, Berkeley, in 2002–2003.

Mal is the founder and chairman of Mal Warwick Associates (Berkeley, California, and Washington, D.C.), a fundraising agency specializing in direct response fundraising and marketing. The company has served nonprofit organizations since 1979. Mal also founded its sister company, Response Management Technologies, a data processing firm for nonprofit organizations, and was a cofounder of the telephone fundraising firm Share Group (Somerville, Massachusetts). In 1999, he cofounded Donordigital (San Francisco), which assists nonprofit organizations with online fundraising, marketing, and advocacy. In 2008, Mal Warwick Associates reacquired Donordigital, and the two firms are now working in tandem to pioneer new approaches in integrated, multichannel fundraising.

Mal has written or edited nineteen books, including the standard fundraising texts, *Revolution in the Mailbox* and *How to Write Successful Fundraising Letters,* both now in second editions. His two books on fundraising strategy—*The Five Strategies for Fundraising Success* and (with Steve Hitchcock) *Ten Steps to Fundraising Success*—are in use throughout the world as strategic planning guides for nongovernmental organizations. He has also coauthored with Ben Cohen *Values-Driven Business: How to Change the World, Make Money, and Have Fun* (Berrett-Koehler, 2006), an introduction to the philosophy and practice of socially responsible business.

Mal is editor of a free monthly electronic newsletter, *Mal Warwick's Newsletter: Successful Direct Mail, Telephone and Online Fundraising,* which has eight thousand subscribers in sixty-nine countries. He is in wide demand throughout the world as a speaker and workshop leader. Mal has taught fundraising on six continents to nonprofit executives from more than a hundred countries. He has spoken annually since 2000 at the International Fundraising Congress (The Netherlands), the International Workshop on Resource Mobilisation (Thailand, Malaysia, and India), the Hemispheric Congress on Fundraising (Mexico), and the Association of Fundraising Professionals' International Conference on Fundraising (United States). He also speaks on the topic of socially responsible business at leading business schools in the United States, as well as for groups of business owners and executives.

Among the hundreds of nonprofits Mal and his colleagues have served over the years are many of the nation's largest and most distinguished charities, as well as six Democratic presidential candidates and scores of small, local, and regional organizations. Collectively, Mal and his associates are responsible for raising at least half a billion dollars, largely in the form of small gifts from individuals.

Mal has played a leadership role in the fundraising and direct marketing fields nationally and internationally. In 2007–2008, he served as chair of the international Resource Alliance (London, U.K.), organizers of the annual International Fundraising Congress in the Netherlands and a leading force globally in developing the fundraising capacity of nongovernmental organizations to build civil society. Having helped establish one of its two predecessor organizations in the early 1980s, he is also an active member of the Direct Marketing Association Nonprofit Federation (Washington, D.C.). He also served for ten years on the board of the Association of Direct Response Fundraising Counsel (Washington, D.C.), two of those years as president.

In 2009, the Direct Marketing Association Nonprofit Federation conferred on Mal the Max Hart Nonprofit Achievement Award "in recognition of career accomplishments by an exceptional fundraising professional with a track record of service, leadership, innovation and integrity."

In 2004, Mal received the Hank Rosso Award as Outstanding Fundraising Executive from the Association of Fundraising Professionals Golden Gate Chapter and Northern California Grantmakers.

Mal also serves on the boards of READ Global (Incline Village, Nevada), which is engaged in sustainable rural development in Nepal and India, and of Great Nonprofits (San Francisco), which is partnering with major institutions to bring the voice of donors and volunteers to the forefront in evaluating the impact of nonprofit organizations. He is a member of the advisory boards of several companies, including Important Gifts (New York, New York) and Mission Research (Lancaster, Pennsylvania).

Mal was a Peace Corps volunteer in Ecuador for more than three years in the 1960s. Since 1969 he has lived in Berkeley, California, where he is deeply involved in local community affairs. Early in the 1990s, he cofounded the

Community Bank of the Bay, the nation's fifth community development bank, and the Berkeley Community Fund, where he served on the board (with one year as its president) until 2006. He also served for eleven years as vice president of the board of the Berkeley Symphony (1991–2002).

In 2006, Mal was awarded the Benjamin Ide Wheeler Medal by the Berkeley Community Fund as "Berkeley's most useful citizen" in recognition of his lifetime contributions to the community. Mal joined environmental leader David Brower, celebrated chef and restaurateur Alice Waters, renowned orchestra conductor Kent Nagano, and other notable Berkeleyans as a recipient of the award.

He is the grandfather of Dayna, Iain, Matthew, Gwen, Andrew, Kaleb, and Benjamin, all of whom live on the East Coast of the United States.

WHEN BAD THINGS HAPPEN TO GOOD CAUSES

I t just ain't fair.

For years now, you've been overworking, or contributing lots of your hard-earned money or spare time, to make the world a better place. You've been attempting to overcome one of humanity's many great challenges: poverty, oppression, ignorance, violence, disease, environmental deterioration. Your work has helped uplift the poor, heal the sick, educate the ill informed, bring dignity to the downtrodden, or restore the environment. There was never enough money, of course, never enough public support, never enough understanding of the importance of your efforts, but somehow you've kept the cause alive, through good times and bad.

Now along come these . . . *people*—these venal real estate speculators, greedy bankers, incompetent or corrupt government officials, money-grubbing hedge fund managers, gnomish international currency traders—whoever they are, wherever they are, *they have screwed up the world economy so badly you can hardly imagine how and when things are ever going to get better again.*

Now, all of a sudden, through no fault of your own—or of anyone you know—your organization's income is trending down, or threatening to do so, and prospects for the months ahead are bleak. Perhaps the endowment's shrinking. Corporate gifts may be drying up. Foundations are pulling back. And even some of your loyal individual donors are giving less, and giving less frequently.

Fundraising When Money Is Tight suggests a way forward—an approach to fundraising for nonprofits that promises to maximize your organization's income in the short term while preserving a foundation for renewed growth once the economic crisis is over.

If you're like so many folks I've spoken to of late, you're probably wondering whether your donors will simply stop giving and you'll be forced to cut your operations to the bone—or worse. In the pages that follow, I explain why I consider that prospect unrealistic. And I describe a course of action that will minimize any damage your organization may suffer as a result of economic conditions.

Please don't get the idea that I'm promising a panacea. As you're well aware, you're likely to feel the pain of the economic crisis regardless of what you do. The economy *will* rise and fall in the future, as will the funding levels of just about every nonprofit organization. And some or all of the steps I spell out in the pages that follow may not be applicable for your organization. In round numbers, there are 1.5 million nonprofit organizations in the United States and 10 million worldwide. Even if you apply a more restrictive definition and count only active, functioning nonprofits with paid staff managing programs dedicated to legitimate educational and charitable purposes, there are tens, perhaps hundreds, of thousands. No straightforward prescription could possibly cure all their financial ills. However, the path I describe should minimize the short-run damage and maximize the long-term potential for nonprofits that have already achieved a high enough degree of diversification in their development programs that they're no longer heavily dependent on one or a handful of donors.

If that's not the case for your organization, or if most of your income is derived from government grants or investments, I doubt that my recommendations will be of much use to you. However, if you receive a meaningful share of your income from individual donors, and especially if there is some variety in the means by which you secure support from the public (through major gifts, legacies, and direct marketing techniques such as direct mail, face-to-face, telemarketing, or online fundraising), then my recommendations in this book will be relevant to you.

• • •

If you read any of the periodicals, online newsletters, or blogs popular among fundraisers, you've probably seen lots of articles with titles similar to that of this book. And if you don't believe that there have been lots of them, take a look at the Reading List at the back of this book. I've actually slogged through all that material, and a lot more besides (especially about business, finance, and the economy in general). Why this book, then?

Although some of the advice I've come across in this reading seems quite good, most of it reads like casual comments quickly thrown together to catch the wave. My colleagues and I at Mal Warwick Associates and Donordigital felt strongly that the all-embracing topic of what has increasingly been called the "economic meltdown" promises to be with us for some time to come and deserved a serious, reasonably in-depth look from the fundraiser's perspective.

There are two overarching aspects of this book that, so far as I can tell, are unique among all the commentaries advanced in the nonprofit sector:

- First, rather than simply react to the crisis, I've treated it as a strategic threat, employing a systematic, scenario-planning approach to envisioning the economic challenges we fundraisers might encounter in the months and years ahead.
- Second, I've gone far enough in depth to cite hundreds of examples and detailed recommendations about the course of action I recommend.

• • •

Fundraising When Money Is Tight is divided into two parts. Part One, "Why You Really Ought to Make Changes in Your Fundraising Program," explores the reasoning I've used to reach my conclusion that there is really only one sure path to both survival in the short term and prosperity in the long. In Part Two, "How You Can Face the Present More Calmly and the Future with Confidence," I spell out the nine steps I suggest you take along that path.

Part One consists of five chapters. In Chapter One, you'll encounter a discussion about what you can learn from economic history. There, I review the literature about the impact of previous recessions, as well as the Great Depression of the 1930s, on giving to nonprofits.

Chapter Two describes a proven way to anticipate the future. Instinctively, we all know that crystal-balling the future is a fool's errand. But there is a proven strategic planning method—widely used by planners in corporate and government circles and in some large nonprofits— that I've put to work in this book. This chapter serves as a brief overview of the technique—not with any intent of teaching you how to do it yourself but simply to explain enough about scenario planning so that the following chapters will make sense to you. (Admittedly, I also hope I'll whet your appetite to learn more about this powerful planning tool.)

Sooner or later, today's economic crisis will come to an end. Chapter Three describes three contrasting economic futures that span the distance from pessimistic to Pollyannish.

Three possible fundraising strategies are set out in Chapter Four. Here, I lead you through three sharply different nonprofit responses to the economic downturn resting on three distinct interpretations of our current reality.

In Chapter Five, you'll see how each of those three contrasting fundraising strategies are likely to play out in each of the three scenarios described earlier. A comparison such as this is the essence of the scenario planning method. Its purpose is to determine whether any of the strategies identified promises optimum results regardless of the scenario. In fact, it will become clear that one of the three strategies appears superior to the others in just about any scenario.

Part Two of this book spells out the components of that strategy in nine chapters.

Chapter Six explores the opportunities you may encounter to tighten up your operations and increase your efficiency.

Strengthening your case for giving is the course I recommend in Chapter Seven. The obvious course—dramatizing to donors how tough times are at your organization—may not be the wisest. Instead, this chapter reviews how to write a powerful and timely case for giving.

In Chapter Eight, I argue—contrary to advice from many other observers—that placing your trust in innovation may make matters worse for your organization, not better. Creativity can be costly, especially when it means spending lots of money to do flashy new things.

Chapter Nine spells out in detail more than two dozen ways you can cut the fat from your fundraising program without sacrificing muscle and bone. You'll find an emphasis on cutting costs in direct marketing, not so much because that happens to have been my specialty for three decades but because direct mail and telemarketing often represent the most expensive aspects of a development program.

In Chapter Ten, I explain how to fish where the big fish are. By making use of simple donor-file segmentation techniques, you can increase your net revenue in the short term while enhancing your prospects over the long haul.

Stay close to your donors. That's the advice I advance in Chapter Eleven, detailing how you can strengthen your existing donor relationships at modest cost and see your revenue rise in the months ahead.

In Chapter Twelve, I show how you can learn more about your donors through a cost-effective, in-house survey technique that will greatly boost your organization's chances of matching your donors' values, beliefs, and goals with the work you do.

Chapter Thirteen offers my advice to step up your efforts online. After explaining that moving most or all of your fundraising efforts to the Internet is *not* the solution to your woes, I spell out more than a dozen concrete suggestions about how to optimize your use of e-mail and the Internet at low cost.

Finally, in Chapter Fourteen, I make the case for integrated, multichannel fundraising—an approach that's especially appropriate in challenging times.

And Chapter Fifteen summarizes these nine practical steps toward peace of mind.

If you really couldn't care less how I've arrived at the recommendations summarized in Chapter Fifteen, skip the first part of the book and start with Chapter Seven. (Just don't tell me you're doing that, because you'll hurt my feelings.)

● ● ●

Fundraising When Money Is Tight could have been written at any time, but I'm writing these words fewer than ninety days after the collapse of Lehman Brothers, the American investment banking firm whose failure is widely credited with triggering the global economic meltdown late in 2008. Charlatans and soothsayers aside, no one can foresee when the current crisis will pass and economic conditions right themselves. To most of us, the immediate future appears grim. It is precisely this uncertainty, and the adverse conditions we fundraisers are already confronting, that convince me this is the ideal time to contemplate how best to organize our fundraising efforts so as to maximize income while money is tight and preserve the capacity to resume growth once a recovery is well under way. Adversity is the best teacher.

The subtitle of this book is *A Strategic and Practical Guide to Surviving Tough Times and Thriving in the Future.* Although I write during what many believe are the toughest of times, I am using the pages of this book to recommend a practical course of action I'm convinced can help your organization suffer the least damage during this or any other economic crisis.

An experienced fundraiser might take a close look at the nine steps I propose in this book and conclude that for the most part, they simply constitute good fundraising. There's truth in that. Much of the advice I advance here is little different from the ideas I've been urging for many years to my clients, in my writing, and on those who attend my workshops and lectures. For decades, I've been emphasizing the importance of donor care, donor research, careful segmentation, and integrated, multichannel fundraising. Nevertheless, I believe that today's economic crisis lends new urgency to these steps.

Equally important, you'll find recommendations in these pages that have been prompted by the current economic meltdown. For example, I've devoted one entire chapter to cost-cutting measures and another to bolstering online fundraising and marketing efforts. I've even counseled cutting back on direct mail testing, the lifeblood of that field. As a dedicated direct marketer, it breaks my heart to do this. But today's uncertain circumstances demand fresh approaches. Sometimes we've got to be ready to roast our sacred cows.

• • •

Writing this book has been rewarding, not just because I've learned so much but also because it has exposed me all over again to the boundless passion and optimism that characterize the social sector. I hope the insight I've gained will prove useful to you too and reinforce your own optimism.

All the best of luck to you! The hopes of humanity for a better future are riding with you.

• • •

Mal Warwick
Berkeley, California
December 2008

Fundraising When Money Is Tight

For Nancy,
who makes it all so easy for me

PART ONE

Why You Really Ought to Make Changes in Your Fundraising Program

It's been awhile now since business as usual was the order of the day. If your organization has been acting as though nothing has changed as the world's economy has stumbled and fallen, it's now long past time to respond to the crisis. And if your organization's leadership has overreacted to conditions and succumbed to panic, it's equally important that you reexamine the world around you and set a course of action grounded in strategic thinking. Part One, comprising five chapters, explores a strategic approach to determining that course.

CHAPTER I

What History Teaches Us

"Onward and upward" appears to be the byword of the human race in the modern era. That's why a massive interruption in the notion of progress, such as the near-collapse of the world's financial systems late in 2008, has been so traumatic.

But history's role is to put things in perspective. A historical view of these matters can help. And the single biggest lesson to be learned from economic historians and economists is that the U.S. economy—and the world's—continues to grow over the long term.

In the United States, the increase in the gross domestic product above the rate of inflation averaged 3.25 percent annually over the 107 years of the twentieth century and the first 7 of the twenty-first. Such seemingly dramatic financial shocks as the OPEC oil embargo in 1973, the collapse of the

U.S. stock market in 1987, or the dot-com bust in 2000—even, ultimately, the crash of 1929—sooner or later come to look like minor setbacks. And, yes, the meltdown of 2008 will eventually be viewed as a hiccup from the vantage point of history. You can see the pattern in Figure 1.1.

Recessions by definition are always temporary. Even depressions, which are much more severe and longer lasting, yield to the long-term trend of economic growth. Of course, sometime later in the twenty-first century, we'll start running out of the resources that fuel economic growth. It's not only oil production that will eventually peak, if it hasn't already. Just as serious are the sharp and continuing declines in the availability of drinkable water and arable land, both of which will be greatly exacerbated by global warming even in the best-case scenario. Eventually the growth curve will flatten

FIGURE 1.1 U.S. Real GDP in Millions of 2000 Dollars

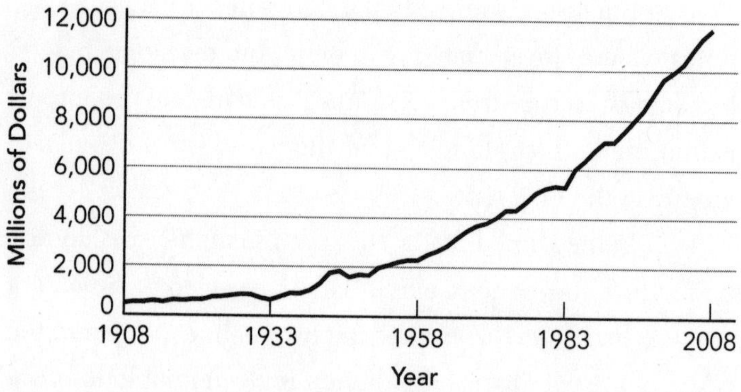

Source: http://www.measuringworth.org/; chart by amCharts.com.

and perhaps turn downward. At that point, humanity may need to dispense with the notion of progress itself, with unknown implications for everything from the way we live to how we think about ourselves. But for the foreseeable future, we can expect any recession that comes along to be followed by a recovery—even, possibly, a rapid one.

Unfortunately, as long as the current recession continues, that statement begs the question: What can we expect from our donors *now*, when money is truly tight?

Philanthropy in Recessionary Times

A growing body of research on fundraising has been pouring out of the Center on Philanthropy at Indiana University as well as other academic centers devoted to the study and advancement of philanthropy. We practitioners might have long memories and anecdotes to spare from decades of experience, but it's the scholars who tap into the raw data increasingly available about fundraising and philanthropy and put our work and our memories into a solid historical framework.

The lesson from the academics is profoundly simple: overall fundraising results roughly correlate with economic conditions, chiefly the trends in personal income and, in the United States, the Standard & Poor's 500 Stock Index (S&P 500). If the economy's up by these measures, fundraising tends to rise. If it's down, fundraising revenue slips.

But this cloud has a lining of silver, or possibly even a platinum one.

According to the Center on Philanthropy, economic reversals during the past four decades have had less of an impact on philanthropy than they have had on the overall economy. Before adjusting for inflation, charitable giving has increased in all years since 1956, with the sole exception of 1987. (Giving actually declined in that year, but just by 1 percent. And the scholars attribute that decline not to economic factors but to a change in the tax laws the previous year that altered the deductibility of charitable gifts.) From 1967 through 2007, the average rate of growth in giving was 2.8 percent in years of economic recession and 4.3 percent in years of economic growth. However, the story is a little different after adjustments for inflation. During the years 1967 to 2007, inflation-adjusted giving fell an average of 1 percent in years of recession. In years when the recession lasted eight months or more, the decline averaged 2.7 percent (again adjusted for inflation).

But we're more interested in the future than the past, right?

The S&P 500 is what economists call a "leading indicator," which means that it tends to predict economic conditions in the near future; fundraising is a "lagging indicator," which means it doesn't slip until a recession is well under way. By the time fundraising results have dropped, the economy may even be on the upswing. And in a mild recession, the recovery may get under way quickly enough to head off any significant decrease in giving—which may help explain the shallow effect of a slow economy on philanthropy.

In addition, economic conditions affect fundraising results in specific ways. The rise and fall of the stock market tends to indicate the ability and willingness of many major foundations and big individual donors to give generous gifts. Foundation grants may be especially prone to drop sharply, since most foundation assets are invested in securities, and foundation boards tend to limit their annual giving to the minimum 5 percent of assets required by law. During previous economic reversals, this effect was also likely to come later than the downturn itself, as grants are typically made on the basis of a three- to five-year average asset evaluation. At worst, foundations tended to allocate funds for the current year in accordance with their asset values at the close of the previous year. In other words, foundations in the past may not have cut back on grant making even in a severe downturn because the value of their assets was still set by an average that included previous boom years. It could take three to five years for the average asset value to decline sharply—and by that point, almost always, the securities markets had resumed their climb.

However, this current recession is like no other economic event in history. Although some foundations are responding to the stress on the nonprofit sector by giving more, many others are pulling back sharply. All bets are off at this writing. But don't take that cautionary news as cause for panic. It would be a mistake to assume that the bottom will drop out just because you're feeling (or fearing) some effects now.

Corporate contributions also tend to shrink as corporate profits decline, and more quickly than at many foundations, although the impact of a poor economy affects different companies in very different ways. Many companies manage to stay profitable through cost cutting even in a down economy. And there are businesses in "countercyclical" industries—ones that serve basic human needs such as groceries that don't go away in a recession—which may even benefit from a downturn and might therefore increase their giving.

Similarly, there are countercyclical effects in the nonprofit sector, helping to explain why a recession doesn't typically hit all nonprofits equally. Difficult economic conditions underline the importance of services for poor people, such as food banks, homeless shelters, and urban missions, reinforcing the case for giving to such traditional charities, while other sectors, such as art museums, performing arts organizations, public broadcasting, and (in the United States) international aid and development, might suffer.

Except in cases of severe economic downturns, the effects tend to be much less pronounced on membership renewal rates, average gifts in direct mail and telefundraising, cash contributions in churches and on the streets, and other barometers of giving by people who aren't necessarily wealthy. It's possible that current demographic changes will eventually moderate or even eliminate that tendency of donors to continue supporting their favorite charities through thick and thin. An aging population that eats up its savings paying for health care is one troubling sign of this potential. Another, its consequences unknown, is the increasing ethnic diversity of the U.S. population. For now, though, I'm banking on what seems to be the boundless generosity of the human race. Nevertheless, as a recession drags on, donor acquisition efforts may become even more challenging than they already are. Even people whose day-to-day finances aren't curtailed by a recession tend to become more cautious, and response rates in new-donor acquisition efforts may shrink because donors hesitate to expand their giving choices. Lower personal income and a bear market in stocks take their toll too.

In summary, here's what to watch out for in any recession:

- An economic downtown may—or may not—adversely affect your fundraising results to any great degree. It depends on the severity, length, and character of the recession.
- Even if nonprofits generally are feeling the pinch of a gloomy economic outlook, your organization might not be similarly affected. The effects you'll feel will depend on how you raise your money, what services you provide, and, ultimately, what you do in response to deteriorating economic conditions.

You may be asking yourself whether this current economic crisis is a recession or something much closer to the protracted economic stagnation of the Great Depression. After all, the impact of most recessions tends to be focused on one country or region at a time, and there's no denying that today's meltdown in the financial markets is a global phenomenon. As I write, it is becoming increasingly clear that this crisis is no mere recession. Its ultimate depth and scope are yet to be seen, but it has already been under way for a full year, and commentators on economics and business are shying away from comparing current conditions to those in any previous economic reversal since World War II. It would seem that the more relevant comparison will prove to be with the Great Depression. What do we know, then, about philanthropy in the 1930s?

Giving During the Depression

During the early years of the Great Depression, according to the limited data we have available, giving did indeed decline significantly three years after the Crash, though not nearly as precipitously as the economy as a whole. Philanthropy then recovered as the 1930s proceeded, even in the absence of significant improvement in economic conditions.

The best information I've been able to locate about philanthropy during the Depression years comes from Robert F. Sharpe Jr., a fundraising consultant widely known for his encyclopedic knowledge of planned giving. A 1991 paper published by the Sharpe Group, re-released in 2008, draws on both the contemporaneous studies of the legendary fundraising consultant John Price Jones beginning in 1931 and a 1950 study by F. Emerson Andrews characterized by the *New York Times* as "the most comprehensive survey of philanthropy ever undertaken in this country" up to that time.

Summing up the overall picture gleaned from these two sources, Sharpe related that

> the Andrews report showed a somewhat significant dip in total giving from 1931–33 at the beginning of the lengthy period of economic stagnation that characterized the 1930s. The report shows a slow annual rise in giving throughout the remainder of the 1930s, a time period when inflation was non-existent—and which might even be characterized as a period of increased giving were deflation of the period factored in.

Viewed graphically, the picture emerges very clearly, as you can see in Figure 1.2.

As you'll note in Figure 1.2, giving didn't begin its decline until 1931–1932, long after the Crash that most people today associate with the onset of the Depression. Although the dollar amount of total contributions did decrease from 1929 to 1931, giving actually rose when adjusted for the inflation (and deflation) that occurred during this time period. Similarly, taking deflation into account, the drop from 1931 to 1933 is not pronounced. (The dollar increased in value from $1.00 in 1929 to $1.33 in 1933.)

**FIGURE 1.2 Inflation-Adjusted
Giving in America, 1929–1941**

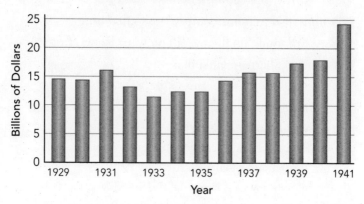

Source: F. Emerson Andrews Sage Foundation Report.

Although it then took a full seven years before the level of giving in America returned to its peak before the onset of the Depression, there were only two years of significant decline (1932 and 1933). The recovery in giving began in 1934—long before the improvement in the overall economy was truly meaningful.

Sharpe notes that the John Paul Jones studies, working from a different set of raw data that was based on more limited surveys, showed a similar pattern. "They reveal, however, a more dramatic drop in initial gift activity from 1931 to 1933" and a recovery to earlier levels that was more erratic than shown in the Andrews study. However, "other more broad-based reports at the time of gifts to Community Chests [the United Ways of yesteryear], Catholic Charities, and others also showed a continuous, though slow, rise in giving each year and tend to corroborate the Andrews study."

Not all nonprofit organizations were equally affected by the Depression. The Sharpe paper reported on a study of giving to higher education that indicated that many colleges and universities—especially the largest and best known—fared relatively well during the 1930s. "Those organizations related to human services, religion, and health care also appeared from contemporary reports to have fared well," the Sharpe Group noted.

During this period, there was another, highly significant trend: "A much higher percentage of individual gift income [was] derived from bequests and deferred gifts during the 1930s, with a return to more normal levels occurring as current giving mushroomed in support of war-related charity."

In other words, during the worst financial crisis in the memory of any living person, there were a couple of significant declines for the nonprofit sector, or at least for most nonprofits. But philanthropy bounced back to pre-Depression levels far more quickly than the world economy in general.

• • •

It's important to weigh this perspective in the balance against the many changes in American philanthropy since the 1930s. A far smaller proportion of the U.S. population then could be counted as donors, so major gifts—and, as Robert Sharpe notes, substantial bequests—constituted a far larger share of overall giving than they do today. Only after World War II did a substantial middle class capable of sharing its prosperity begin to dominate the American economy. Direct mail fundraising—mass fundraising of all sorts—didn't begin coming into its own until the late 1940s. The number of charitable foundations was a tiny fraction of the more than 100,000 in the United States today. There were no computers, no Internet, no e-mail. Still, the fact that giving was less sharply hit than the economy as a whole seems relevant. The same pattern has prevailed through every subsequent economic downturn. It appears as though the philanthropic impulse is stimulated, not discouraged, by the widespread evidence of growing need during difficult times.

If the fundamental question at hand remains simply whether today's economic troubles constitute a recession (mild or otherwise) rather than a severe reversal that economists would call a depression, why don't we just put on our thinking caps, using all the magical devices in the economists' toolbox, and determine what's in store for us?

Since you already know that crystal-balling the future is a fool's errand, we'll take a look in the following chapter about a tested and proven method to anticipate—not predict—the future.

CHAPTER 2

A Proven Way to Anticipate the Future

More than a hundred years ago, in the closing years of the nineteenth century, our cities were choked with coal dust, factories ran on steam power, the horse was the dominant mode of transportation, and epidemic disease ran rampant across the globe. Who could foresee a future with electricity in our homes, our roads and streets clogged with gasoline-powered vehicles, and smallpox eradicated?

Not Charles H. Duell, commissioner of the U.S. Patent Office, who famously said in 1899 that "everything that can be invented has been invented." The man actually proposed to the U.S. Congress that it shut down the Patent Office because it would no longer be needed!

Duell wasn't alone. Experts routinely fail to predict major changes. Even meteorologists armed with supercomputers can't reliably predict next week's weather.

Clearly, humankind's track record in envisioning its future has been extremely poor. Dramatic failures have been the rule, not the exception.

As I write these words, I sit in a hotel room in Mombasa, Kenya, on the shore of the Indian Ocean, many thousands of miles from the world's economic centers in New York, London, Frankfurt, and Hong Kong. The impact of the current economic meltdown is less obvious here than it was back home in California, where home foreclosure signs dotted the landscape, but the effects are unmistakable nonetheless. Prices of export commodities are slumping as world trade begins to shrink, and thousands of Kenyan tea and coffee farmers face the likely prospect of destitution for months, and perhaps years, ahead.

If anyone here in East Africa envisioned these current economic conditions, I would be mightily surprised. I know professional investment managers actively engaged in the New York financial markets on a daily basis who hadn't a clue the current meltdown was coming. So could you imagine that any of us, no matter how well connected or knowledgeable about finance and economic affairs, could possibly predict our economic future?

Of course not! So let's take a look instead at a method proven to be useful in anticipating the unforeseeable—a strategic planning tool familiar to corporate and government planners that's known as scenario planning.

How Scenario Planning Works

Scenario planning is not an exercise in figuring out what's most likely to happen next year, or three years from now, or five. It is a strategic planning method expressly developed to test the viability of alternative strategies.

Using scenario planning, Royal Dutch-Shell, for decades one of the world's two biggest oil companies, outclassed its competition, including hundreds of smaller and presumably much nimbler corporations:

- The petroleum market is notoriously difficult to predict. Yet Shell foresaw the precedent-shattering 1973–1974 OPEC oil embargo in advance. It was the only major oil company that had a clue—and it made a bundle on that prediction.
- Something similar occurred at Shell in the 1980s. Because some of the biggest oil reserves in the world lay within the borders of the Soviet Union, what happened there mattered a lot to the petroleum industry. Royal Dutch-Shell defied all the Soviet experts—including the CIA and just about every other national intelligence service—in anticipating several years in advance the breakup of the Soviet Union. Once again, the company gained a substantial advantage over its competitors.

I'll admit it: scenario planning isn't simple. It requires analytical skills, a broad range of knowledge, a disciplined group of people who work well together, and, frequently, a lot of time. But for those who persist and succeed, the rewards can be rich indeed.

To learn more about the scenario planning method, I suggest you start with Peter Schwartz's classic 1991 book, *The Art of the Long View*. Because Schwartz has done so much better a job than I could at explaining how the method works, I won't attempt to duplicate his work here. I'll simply describe the process in general so you can understand how I arrived at the recommendations in the chapters that follow.

The scenario planning process has six simple steps.

Step 1: Determine the Fundamental Question at Issue

Start by figuring out the biggest question your organization will have to face in the future. As Schwartz puts it, what is it that keeps you awake nights?

Let's consider the prospects for fundraising in the throes of a severe economic downturn. Isn't the question we're all grappling with whether our donors will simply stop giving and we'll be forced to cut our operations to the bone — or worse?

If this is indeed the central question, we now know what this particular scenario planning exercise is all about. This will permit us to conduct a series of discussions that bear less resemblance to sophomoric dormitory bull sessions and focus instead on what's really most important to the organizations and institutions we care so much about.

Step 2: Figure Out What You Don't Know

Once you've got a handle on the Big Question, sit down and figure out the things you need to learn in order to take a crack at answering the question. These further questions—the things you don't know until you check them out—are called *strategic uncertainties*. You may have to do some research. You certainly *will* need to do a lot of thinking.

First, list the factors that your leadership must take into account in answering the strategic question you've posed. What are the strategic uncertainties? In an economic downturn, those factors might include at least the following:

- How long the recession will last
- How deeply the recession will affect our clients or beneficiaries
- The impact on our institutional funders (foundations, trusts, and corporations)
- How our individual donors will be affected

If you're doing a good job, you'll come up with lots of questions. The next task is to figure out which of these strategic uncertainties are the most important ones *in the light of the decision you have to make.* Pick just three or four to avoid getting muddled. That calls for judgment—but, hey, that's why they pay you the big bucks, isn't it?

Step 3: Gather the Necessary Information

If you're an active, aware citizen, you're constantly gathering information. You read newspapers, magazines, and books. You catch the news on TV, on radio, or on the Web. You talk to people in many walks of life—at work, on the street, and in your social life. All the general knowledge you accumulate in the normal course of your life is essential as you embark on scenario planning. But it's not enough.

To ponder how the economy will affect your organization's financial health next year and in the years ahead, you'll need to do a lot more reading. You may also have to consult a qualified economist. Be careful, though. Don't overdo it. Decision makers in every field constantly warn that they "never have enough information." Don't let the research process drag on so long that the question becomes moot before you complete your analysis.

Step 4: Determine How Broad Trends in Society Might Influence Your Decision

Analyze what scenario planners call the *driving forces*—the factors that can make a life-or-death difference in the way things turn out. They're the Big Picture events and activities that have the potential to upend our lives overnight—to make the world a different place. These driving forces include the following four categories (at a minimum):

- Social dynamics
- Economic forces
- Political issues
- Technological developments

These are factors that could affect any or all of us. In practice, scenario planners look into each of these categories in depth, one at a time. I'll just leave it that I've pondered these questions and based what follows in this book in part on the conclusions I reached about them.

Now comes the fun part. This is where you get to tell stories.

Step 5: Write Several Sharply Contrasting Stories to Illustrate What the World Will Look Like If the Worst—or the Best—Happens

These stories, or scenarios, will portray possible—but perhaps unlikely—futures. For example, one story may represent the state of things to come if some current major trend continues unchecked; another if some unanticipated change, perhaps political or technological, reshuffles the deck of reality; a third if "things just keep getting worse"; and a fourth if "things pretty much stay the same as they are."

If you work at this task as a group, you'll come up with a bunch of scenarios. But a bunch is too many. You'll need to settle on two, three, or at most four scenarios if you're to have any hope of understanding, much less explaining, the consequences of the strategic choices you face.

So, next, merge or modify the scenarios you've constructed. Select two or three significantly different portrayals of the future. As you'll see in the next chapter, that's exactly what I've done in arriving at three sketches of our immediate economic future.

Having envisioned these possible (if improbable) futures, the scenario planning team at each organization will carefully review the consequences they anticipate from each scenario in the event that it proves valid.

Step 6: Test Strategic Choices in Light of These Contrasting Scenarios

Once you've written your stories and pondered their potential impact on your organization, it's time to try answering that big strategic question you started with. Use "what-if" reasoning to think through the consequences of the alternative choices you face. Consider how each strategic choice will play out in each of the scenarios you've constructed.

The objective here is to test how well a given strategic choice will hold up in two or more alternative futures. Don't worry if these "futures" seem unbelievable, or even a little silly. If you've done a good job writing scenarios, you'll have two or three stories that represent the extreme possibilities the future holds. If a particular strategic choice looks as though it ought to hold up better than other choices—no matter which scenario proves closest to the truth—then you may have saved the day (not today, but the day after tomorrow).

That's the line of approach I'll take in Chapter Five.

•••

Now that you have a passing acquaintance with the scenario planning method, follow me into Chapter Three, where I'll put the method to use in an effort to anticipate our economic future. Use Table 2.1 as your guide to the scenario planning process.

TABLE 2.1 Summary of the Scenario Planning Process

Step	Description	Example
1. What is the question?	What is it that keeps you awake nights?	Will giving drop precipitously in the recession?
2. What *don't* you know?	What are the strategic uncertainties about which you need more information?	How long will the recession last? How severe will it be? How badly will nonprofits be affected?
3. Gather the necessary information.	Read, research, consult, confer.	Learn more about recession economics and the history of giving.
4. Explore broad trends.	Study and discuss social dynamics, economic forces, political issues, technological developments.	Consider the potential impact of legislation encouraging philanthropy and volunteerism.
5. Write stories.	Explore contrasting futures through fictional depictions of imagined trends and their intersection.	What happens if the recession ends quickly, drags on for awhile, or deepens into a long depression?
6. Test strategic choices.	Consider how each of several alternative strategies will play out in the context of each of the scenarios you've written.	How well would your chosen strategy fare if the recession ends quickly, drags on for awhile, or deepens into a long depression?

CHAPTER 3

Three Scenarios for Economic Recovery

Somehow we humans, or at least those of us in a position to wield big shovels, have dug ourselves into quite a big economic hole. The question is, how—and when—are we going to dig our way out of it?

Simple logic suggests that, broadly speaking, there are three possible financial futures in store for us—exit strategies, if you will:

- *Things get better quickly.* If you displayed the principal economic indicators on a chart, the resulting curve would look a whole lot like a "V." In the course of one year or less, what went down suddenly starts going back up again, reflecting the volatility that has become the dominant characteristic of the world's financial markets. This would be scenario A, "Happy Times Are Here Again."

- *Things stay more or less the same as they are at this writing, which is to say they're really rotten.* But gradually the economic indicators bottom out, and then, month by month, they steadily get better. The whole process requires no more than three years at the outside. On a chart, the curve formed would resemble a "U." We'll call this scenario B, "On the Road Again."

- *Things get worse and stay that way for a long time:* three years, five years, seven or more. (By some measures, the Great Depression lasted a full decade.) The curve on the chart resembles an "L," which is how some people refer to the lengthy period of decline and stagnation in the Japanese economy throughout the 1990s and the first three years of the new century. Let's call that scenario C, or "Misery Loves Company."

Let's take a look at each of these three alternative futures and how they might affect our work as fundraisers and the health of the organizations and institutions we serve.

Scenario A: Happy Days Are Here Again

Stephanie was one of those people whose family, friends, and colleagues at work frequently asked for financial advice. Even before the meltdown of 2008, her investments had always seemed to do well. She had even anticipated the market collapse, selling stocks and going heavily into cash early that year. Now, just over a year later, she was considering the possibility of buying back in. She knew, though, that it wouldn't be wise to reenter the market too soon, since that was such a common error among small investors. She'd test the waters maybe in a few more months. It was a foolish error to chase the bottom of the market—or the top. In any case, Stephanie was no small investor anymore. After a decade in a top executive position, pulling down a salary well into six figures, she had probably socked away enough to retire anytime she wished. Retirement was the furthest thing from her mind, however. Not yet out of her forties, Stephanie still stirred with ambition. After all, those letters "CEO" would look really good after her name!

Until a few years ago, Stephanie had never thought much about supporting nonprofit causes. Something of a workaholic, she rarely thought about anything at all but work. But her mentor had made it clear that getting ahead in the corporate world meant giving a little here and there, demonstrating support for her community and the sort of social conscience that boards now seemed to be seeking in top executives. And, she had to admit, now that she'd reached her mid-forties, she was starting to wonder about what she'd really accomplished in life so far. That made it a lot easier for Stephanie to take her mentor's advice. Thus it was that, shortly afterward, Stephanie made generous gifts to the local art museum and ballet company, and she volunteered to head up the company's annual United Way campaign. Since then, she'd been giving somewhat more generous gifts to each of these three institutions on an annual basis without fail. The meltdown in the economy hadn't touched her, so there was no reason not to do so.

Stephanie wasn't alone. As the economic downturn began visibly leveling off, the news was starting to feature stories about people like Stephanie who'd actually profited from the meltdown of 2008.

Proving once again that fear can feed on itself and reach truly irrational levels, all signs in October 2009 point to renewed economic growth following less than two years of what economists were now calling a "protracted but manageable recession." Decisive government action, much of it internationally coordinated for the first time in history, is credited with the predicted turnaround.

After lukewarm year-end fundraising results for non-profits in 2008 and discouraging news that continued well into the spring of 2009, giving is now clearly on the rise. The widely feared collapse in foundation giving and major gifts has not materialized since financial markets stabilized in 2009, restoring trillions in lost investment value. Response to direct marketing appeals, which was better than expected in December and January, is returning to historically more familiar levels. Even response rates in direct mail donor acquisition efforts, long the weakest link in the direct marketing chain, are looking healthier. A similar pattern prevails throughout North America, Europe, Australia, and Hong Kong.

Scenario B: On the Road Again

George doesn't think of himself as a donor. So far as he's concerned, a donor is one of those rich, stuffy, old people who get wings in art museums and buildings on college campuses named after them. George is an activist. For several years now, he's been giving small amounts of money each month to several human rights and civil liberties organizations. About a year ago, when a rumor was going around the office that job cuts might be on the way, George ended his monthly gifts to an environmental group he particularly admired, and he cut back on a couple of the other organizations. But now that things are looking up, he's ready to resume his full support for them.

Though George isn't aware of it, the pattern of his giving is typical of that shown by millions of people who kept their jobs through the downturn, despite the ever-present threat of unemployment. Clearly that threat has forced many of these people to be far more cautious than they'd been in earlier years. They've used their credit cards far more sparingly, postponed major expenditures such as foreign travel or additions to the house, and reduced their giving to nonprofit causes and institutions, just as George has. But times are changing again.

It's late in 2010, and at last the proverbial light is shining brightly at the end of the economic tunnel. In the United States, the S&P 500 has been moving steadily upward for months now, anticipating—and reinforcing—the psychological impact of steadily more positive reports of reduced unemployment, stabilizing wages, and recovering export revenues. Most observers credit the turnaround to the resolute action of the Obama administration, which invested unprecedented sums in reviving consumer confidence and keeping the country's financial infrastructure from total collapse.

In many developing economies, conditions are still grim, but the leading U.S. trade partners—Canada, Mexico, Japan, China, and the European Union—are showing strong signs of renewed economic health. Joblessness is on the decline, businesses are making capital investments once again, and consumers are spending their money more freely. Leading securities indexes in financial markets across the planet are pointing upward after two years of a painful bear market.

After a period of stagnation in 2009 and early 2010, philanthropic revenues are rising in response to the brighter economic outlook, renewed consumer confidence, and rising personal income. The more venturesome observers of the nonprofit sector are now predicting a strong year-end finish for the nation's nonprofits, and an even brighter year ahead in 2011. The worst is past.

Scenario C: Misery Loves Company

For most of her long life, Karen has been a generous donor—not giving as much as some, because she could hardly be called truly rich, but still entirely respectable amounts. Her giving reflects a life-long commitment to share her good fortune and to "make a difference." Karen cares deeply about the problems of poverty and the environment, and her steady contributions to several leading nonprofit organizations have clearly reflected that concern. But she has been forced by conditions beyond her control to curtail her giving sharply during the last couple of years. No longer can she contribute generously to the dozen organizations she favored. She's been forced to cut that number in half, and even to cut back on the amounts she gives to the six that she still actively supports. Things don't look any better for next year or the following one either. Karen's retirement funds, and the generous income she received for many years, have shrunk to no more than one-third their previous value. Karen can no longer be considered "comfortable."

There's only one way left for Karen to help the causes she cares so much about: legacy giving. Unlike most of her contemporaries, Karen passed the age of sixty without ever having drawn up a will. After all, with no children and no other immediate family still alive, she hadn't seriously considered what would happen to her assets when she died. In 2009, though, as Karen began to despair of her shrinking contributions to her favorite organizations, a magazine article about an old friend who'd left millions to the local college suddenly made her realize that she too could will her home and the value remaining in her savings and retirement account to the nonprofit organizations she favored the most. It gives her a feeling of comfort knowing that when she eventually passes away, they'll receive what is, after all, a rather tidy sum, even after the market declines of the past three years.

It's 2012, and economic conditions worldwide continue to be gloomy. The bugaboo of inflation has long since receded, with prices for many products falling steadily in the face of continually declining demand and flagging world trade. Deflation is the order of the day. The U.S. economy is struggling to contain unemployment at 14 percent—far short of the 25 percent it reached in the Great Depression, but punishing millions nonetheless. In Europe and East Asia, the jobless rolls are bulging. Companies large and small are going bankrupt at record rates, compounding the challenge for governments whose resources prove inadequate to revive consumer spending and keep credit flowing.

Viewed in historical terms, stock markets around the world are hovering near their all-time lows, though optimists read the signs as pointing to economic recovery within two to three years. Optimists are few and far between, though. The protracted bear market in securities reflects bad news quickly while giving short shrift to the occasional positive development.

Worldwide, the poor suffer the most, as is always the case. With export prices sharply down in goods of all types—minerals, agricultural products, textiles, electronics—factories are shuttered and jobless rural immigrants wander the streets of megacities throughout the Global South. Millions who had begun to move to the margins of the middle class in the opening years of the twenty-first century are slipping back into poverty. Hunger is spreading, and with it, epidemic disease.

Giving USA 2012 is widely expected to disclose the fourth consecutive annual drop in American philanthropic revenue. Recent reports from the United Way, the American Red Cross, and other prominent nonprofits suggest the falloff in total giving may be as much as 15 percent, equaling or even exceeding last year's record decline. Last year, for the first time ever, the number of nonprofit organizations registered under Section 501(c)(3) actually shrank, and that trend is predicted to accelerate this year, as the accumulated impact of three years' declining revenues takes its inevitable toll.

According to researchers at Johns Hopkins University, Henley Management College, Indiana University, and elsewhere, a similar pattern prevails in Europe, Canada, Australia, Hong Kong, and other parts of the world where civil society has taken firm hold and the habit of philanthropy has become widespread. For the social sector, no less than for business, money is indeed tight, and no end to the crisis is in sight.

● ● ●

The impact of any one of these three scenarios will differ greatly from one organization to another. The ability of any nonprofit to survive tough times, regardless of how severe economic conditions may be, will vary for many reasons. On the positive side:

- Well-established institutions such as major colleges and universities will see their endowments shrink, and they may well be forced to trim or even cut back their operations. However, it's highly unlikely any of them will face the prospect of bankruptcy. Any nonprofit organization or institution with substantial financial reserves possesses the capacity to withstand even a major economic reversal.

- Nonprofit organizations that deliver tangible, immediate, and local survival services such as food banks and homeless shelters may be forced to do more with less, but they're in a strong position to mobilize public support.

- Organizations that champion children and animals are likely to face the least difficulty raising money in tough times. Any truly popular cause will be better positioned than one that's controversial.

- Established brand names command a premium in difficult times as they have less to prove to a demanding public. In general, nonprofit organizations that have been in business for decades and have substantial numbers of donors are far more likely to endure through an economic crisis than those that have been recently established, have poor name recognition, and possess relatively few donors.

By contrast, some nonprofits will find themselves at a severe disadvantage whether the economic slump endures for years or just months:

- Any organization whose vision, mission, and values are unfocused and difficult for outsiders to understand is likely to suffer. If there are fundamental weaknesses in a nonprofit's case for giving, a recession will exacerbate them.
- Any nonprofit that was already having trouble raising money before the recession may find that tough times only increase donors' resistance. If the organization's fundraising and marketing efforts are poorly executed, the price it will pay during tough times will be all the greater.
- Nonprofit organizations that have been living from month to month may be in trouble. And if an organization's continued existence hangs on the renewal of a single major gift or foundation grant, its future is highly uncertain.
- Organizations that depend heavily on the largesse of wealthy donors are also likely to experience tough sledding. Institutions such as art museums, symphony orchestras, ballet and theater companies, and other favorites of the cultural elite may be well enough established and have sufficient reserves to weather a difficult era. They're likely to suffer, though.
- During tough times, most people tend to focus on what's closest to home. At least in the United States, where support for international aid and development has never been widely popular, nonprofits with an international focus may find themselves at a disadvantage.

Despite these distinctions from one organization to another, it's important for us all to ponder which of the three scenarios—Happy Days, On the Road, or Misery—will prevail. We live in a networked world where none of us is fully immune to the troubles that befall others.

• • •

These three scenarios represent the logical extremes of the future we may expect to unfold. They're not predictions. They're landscapes against which we can examine a range of possible options for fundraising strategy as this (or any other) economic crisis drags on. So for simplicity, let's examine how three different approaches to fundraising might fare in each of these scenarios—approaches we might characterize as Defensive, Selective, and Aggressive.

CHAPTER 4

Three Possible Fundraising Strategies

I n the previous chapter, we examined three alternative scenarios for our economic future, an exercise in visioning
that provides a backdrop against which we can examine a
range of possible approaches to fundraising. Now let's look at
three significantly distinct strategies that we might pursue as
this economic crisis, or any other economic crisis, continues
without letup.

Strategy 1: The Defensive Approach

Both the board and the executive director are convinced
beyond argument that the economic meltdown represents a
mortal threat to HumanCare's survival. The endowment has
already shriveled by nearly half, foundation commitments
once thought firm now seem shaky, and a major corporate

sponsorship appears increasingly unlikely despite the company's continued reassurance that they'll weather the storm. Ongoing contributions from individual donors are declining. The executive committee, and then the board as a whole, therefore has mandated the following guidelines for the development department:

- Cost cutting is paramount. Discontinue any marginal program activities, and reduce staff accordingly. Opportunities to outsource or eliminate noncore activities must be pursued immediately.
- Immediately shift funds from the investment portfolio into cash accounts to prevent additional losses from the collapsing securities market.
- End direct mail and face-to-face donor acquisition activities at the earliest possible moment permitted by donor stipulations and contractual obligations. Recruiting new donors costs money—a lot of it—and this is no time to be spending money unless it's absolutely essential to do so. After all, what harm can come if donor acquisition goes on the back burner for a year or two?
- The name of the game in donor development must be cost-effectiveness. Every activity conducted by the development staff has to be justified by an immediate return on investment. This means eliminating thank-you letters, or at the very least replacing those previously personalized gift acknowledgments with preprinted post cards.

(Surely, our donors will understand the need for cost cutting at this critical time, won't they?)

- To save more money, reduce the frequency of donor appeals, and cut back from five membership renewal notices to four or even three. For those direct mail and telemarketing projects that get the green light, reduce quantities to cut costs further. Cancel all marginally profitable special events, and be prepared to throw in the towel on the annual gala dinner if it proves difficult, as anticipated, to secure the necessary sponsorships.
- Bring gift processing and donor file maintenance in-house, redirecting staff members formerly employed in the direct marketing department and special events to work temporarily in the new back office, to minimize the number of layoffs necessary in the development department.

By taking these admittedly radical steps, HumanCare hopes to weather what the leadership sees as the second Great Depression in a century.

Strategy 2: The Selective Approach

Save the Earth has long been one of the most celebrated environmental organizations, operating in more than sixty countries from its home base in the United States. Its president and CEO takes special pride in Save the Earth's enormous grassroots membership, which she played no small part in building in her previous position as the group's director of membership and fundraising. The economic crisis that has come on so suddenly and so fiercely was a shock, of course, but the senior management team early on resolved to take a judicious approach, avoiding hasty action they might later regret. On the initiative of the CEO and with unanimous backing from senior management, the board of Save the Earth has determined to put in place the following principles and guidelines for the next six months:

- Reassess all programs from top to bottom to ensure that marginal activities are cut back (if necessary for future growth or to meet contract requirements) or entirely eliminated. Shift staff to more productive activities in order to preserve jobs and minimize the costs of training new employees.
- Undertake an immediate review with outside counsel of the investment portfolio. Shift funds as necessary to reduce the risk of further losses.
- Strengthen the case for giving to match the reality of the times. Announce to donors the measures Save the Earth has put in place to save costs, minimize waste, and trim less productive activities. Demonstrate how the financial crisis is making matters worse for the environment, increasing poaching of endangered species in poor countries, discouraging home owners and businesspeople from investing in solar retrofits and other energy-saving

methods, and causing institutional funders all over the world—foundations and trusts, corporations, even governments and intergovernmental agencies—to invest less in environmental initiatives. The crisis adds urgency to the cause, greatly increasing the value of ongoing support from loyal members.

- Set ambitious new goals for major gift and planned giving officers to spend more time face-to-face with their donors and prospects. Enlist willing members of the board to join in the effort and provide additional support staff if necessary. Ensure that all major donors are contacted personally within three to four months and brought fully up-to-date on how Save the Earth is responding to the crisis.

- Maximize net revenue in the short term. Economize on such fair-weather activities as nonessential direct mail testing, costly cultivation events, and glossy magazines or newsletters. Show the members and the rest of the world that Save the Earth is frugal about spending money, and make sure they get the message. Fine-tune segmentation in direct mail and telemarketing to remove lapsed and long-lapsed members from most special appeals and renewals. Examine the cost-effectiveness of the front-end premiums used in the direct mail program, economizing where possible to reduce costs and boost net revenue.

- Make the greatest possible use of online communications to recruit new supporters at low cost, reinforce messages to members and the public conveyed through other channels, and convert online activists to members. Accelerate the process of weaning members from Save the Earth's printed newsletter to an electronic version.
- Maintain the long-term value of the donor base, and enhance it if possible. Avoid canceling in-house solicitations, whether special appeals or renewals. Instead, increase the frequency of solicitations to donors who normally generate high net revenue. Resist the temptation to economize on the member acknowledgment program. Instead, step up gift acknowledgments and donor cultivation activities to strengthen relationships with members. Find low-cost ways to learn more about the most loyal and generous donors, and integrate new information into personalized appeals to them.
- Review the member acquisition program with great care. Examine the long-term value of members, ranking the acquisition lists from which they came and favoring with reorders those lists that come out on top. Cut back on or avoid lists that are entirely marginal when measured by the long-term value of the members they've produced in the past.

In this deliberative fashion, the leadership of Save the Earth believes the organization stands the best chance of maximizing short-term income while preserving the capacity to resume its impressive growth once the economic crisis has passed.

Strategy 3: The Aggressive Approach

The glass is half full as far as the majority of the board of Angel House is concerned. The debate over the hospice's response to the economic meltdown has been dominated by its wealthiest member, a self-styled contrarian who has made a huge fortune in the stock market and is impossible to ignore. As he argued, the hospice has always managed to marshal the financial support needed to maintain its high-quality services. His contagious optimism convinces both his fellow board members and the management staff that there will be new fundraising opportunities during this recession. While other charities head for the hills, canceling appeals and treating their donors with great caution, Angel House will expand its donor base. The approach the board and CEO elect to take is straightforward:

- Pull out all the stops to take advantage of the opportunity created by what they view as the undue caution their competitors are exhibiting. Step up donor acquisition activities by mail and online, even knowing that response rates may be lower than in the past—but hoping that so many organizations will be eliminating their own donor acquisition activities that response may even improve. In any case, surely the investment will pay off in the long run, as it always has.

- Launch a new major donor campaign themed to match the times, a "Campaign for the Future" to demonstrate that Angel House plans to stay in business for a long time to come, economic crisis or not. Push hard for more and bigger gifts from donors while maintaining current stewardship policies without change.

- On the assumption that the decline in securities prices will persuade donors that gifts of securities will no longer cost them so much, include an appeal for gifts of securities as part of the Campaign for the Future.

- Accelerate plans for the annual gala dinner, knowing that several local charities have already canceled plans to hold theirs. Reach out aggressively for new sponsors among the city's cultural elite.

- Innovate actively, testing new direct mail packages and new appeals online. Experiment with keyword buys at Google and other search engines, append e-mail addresses to the existing Angel House donor list, and invest in a short animated video feature in hopes of reaching a much wider audience through viral pass-alongs. Move actively into the leading social networking sites, and heavily promote the Angel House pages there among the donors.

This is the approach that Angel House will take in its development program as the months unfold. It's betting the ranch on its optimism.

• • •

Three distinctly different strategies. Which one comes closest to the course your organization should follow? To gain insight into how these strategies might fare in disparate circumstances, let's try out each of them in turn against the backdrop of the three scenarios sketched out in Chapter Three. That's the business of the following chapter.

CHAPTER 5

Identify a Winning Strategy

This is the part where push comes to shove.

In Chapter Three, we explored three economic scenarios for the months and years ahead, viewing three donors whose attitudes and circumstances were emblematic of the times. Then, in Chapter Four, we took a look at three hypothetical nonprofit organizations and the fundraising strategies they elected to pursue in response to the economic conditions they anticipated. Now we'll examine the likely results when each of the three broadly defined strategies is implemented in each of the three scenarios.

For an overview of this exercise, see Table 5.1. There, you'll find each of the three scenarios described in Chapter

TABLE 5.1 Finding a Winning Strategy

Scenario	Defensive Approach	Selective Approach	Aggressive Approach
A. Happy Days Are Here Again	Survival—by the skin of your teeth	Nothing lost but a little time	Hindsight is delicious
B. On the Road Again	Nothing ventured, nothing gained	Poised for growth again	Get ready to count your losses
C. Misery Loves Company	Survival—but not for long	Count your blessings	This means bankruptcy

Four row by row on the left-hand side. The three strategies I explored constitute the three columns to the right.

Consequences of Pursuing the Defensive Approach

As you can see in the table, the Defensive Approach will ensure that a nonprofit survives only the early stages of a truly severe economic downturn (scenario C, "Misery Loves Company"). In scenario B, "On the Road Again," the Defensive Approach suggests that an organization will fall behind its competitors as conditions improve. In scenario A, a defensive strategy is a prescription for decline as less fearful nonprofits pull steadily ahead.

Not convinced? Consider what HumanCare could realistically expect if it pursued the approach it elected. In uncertain economic times—especially when the airwaves and the front pages are abuzz with talk of recession—nonprofit executives may overreact, which is precisely what the leadership of HumanCare has done. Under pressure from the board of directors, the professional staff has taken cost cutting too far. Recall that for HumanCare, the Defensive Approach means that new-donor acquisition will cease, and donor cultivation programs such as donor acknowledgments will be cut back severely. These are the easiest targets, but in many ways the most unfortunate. Witness, for example, the impact of a one-year hiatus in donor acquisition imposed on a growing direct mail donor development program

The chart shown in Figure 5.1 illustrates the difference in cumulative revenue received over five years with

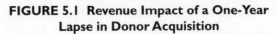

FIGURE 5.1 Revenue Impact of a One-Year Lapse in Donor Acquisition

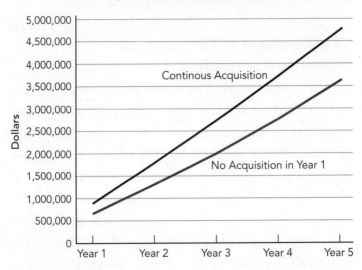

either no change in donor acquisition volume or a suspension of acquisition in Year 1. It's based on a growing direct mail program with 8,000 active donors who contributed $1 million last year. Typically this program acquires 2,500 new donors a year to sustain its growth. New donors contribute little revenue in their first year on the file (and must be acquired at a loss), but their long-term contribution to revenue within five years is over $1 million, a critical amount for a program of this scale. How can this possibly happen? By refraining from acquiring any new donors in Year 1, as compared to 2,500 the previous year, the organization's donor file shrinks through natural attrition rather than grows. Thus, there may be a total active donor file in Year 2 of fewer than 7,000 donors rather than 9,500. Those 2,500 extra donors could account for one-quarter of total revenue in Year 2 and generate increasing amounts of revenue in subsequent years.

Curtailing donor acknowledgment activities in the guise of cost cutting can be similarly counterproductive. Eliminating or economizing on thank-you letters or phone calls will prove to be a major error over the long term. Renewal rates will slip, donor loyalty will decrease, and the donor base will eventually shrink. And if such cost-cutting steps are combined with a cutback in donor acquisition, the result can be tragic.

Now let's review the consequences of pursuing the Aggressive Approach.

Results of the Aggressive Approach

In scenario C, "Misery Loves Company," the Aggressive Approach is a formula for bankruptcy. It won't take a lot of number crunching for the staff and board of Angel House to prove to themselves that if new donor acquisition costs rise from, say, $25 per donor to $50 or $100, its available capital will be exhausted in short order. They'll also likely find that big investments in direct mail testing, online social networking, and other normally risky activities will drain available funds too. A full-blown depression is no time to indulge creative urges.

Should the financial environment look more like the scenario we've entitled "On the Road Again" (scenario B),

Angel House's aggressive strategy will guarantee losses in the near term, perhaps substantial ones—for the same reasons and in the same ways as they do in scenario C. Bankruptcy may not be the result if the hospice's financial reserves hold out long enough, but there is no question Angel House will be greatly weakened after a year, or even six months, and will find itself at a competitive disadvantage once the recession ends.

Only under scenario A, "Happy Days Are Here Again," will Angel House's Aggressive Approach appear wise in hindsight, and that contrarian on its board will prove to have been prescient. Still, was it worthwhile for his colleagues to take this risk? How much money would you have wagered in the early months of 2009 that the recession ushered in by the meltdown of 2008 would abruptly end within a few months?

What Happens with the Selective Approach?

By contrast with both the defensive and the aggressive strategies, the Selective Approach appears to maximize Save the Earth's chances of surviving, even flourishing, regardless of the direction the overall economy takes.

In scenario C, "Misery Loves Company," the organization's cost-cutting efforts, combined with continuing emphasis on stewardship, keep the organization in business for the near term and strong for the long run. Its donor base remains intact, stable, or (at worst) only slightly smaller than at the outset of the depression. Most of its committed donors, coddled by Save the Earth's persistent stewardship practices, have sustained their giving levels, and many have increased their support to help the organization meet the growing need for its work.

For scenario B, "On the Road Again," the Selective Approach preserves Save the Earth's capacity to resume growth as the economy gradually improves. Funds saved by careful cost-cutting measures can now be invested in an expanded donor acquisition program, even in such areas of long-term investment as social networking experiments.

In scenario A, "Happy Days Are Here Again," with conditions rapidly stabilizing, the Selective Approach leaves Save the Earth with the resources to shift strategy as the dire predictions of depression prove unfounded. Having taken only those cost-cutting steps that were absolutely necessary, Save the Earth is able to shift gears quickly as the economy approaches equilibrium.

• • •

Thus, only one of these three broadly construed strategies—what I've termed the Selective Approach—appears to hold promise under almost any foreseeable economic circumstances:

- The Defensive and Aggressive Approaches lead to disaster in at least one of the three scenarios. If you pursue one of those strategies and you guess wrong about the direction the economy takes, you're in trouble. Maybe very deep trouble if your organization's finances are anything but completely solid to begin with.

- If the Defensive Approach entails laying off staff, it will be difficult and probably time-consuming to replace them once the recovery begins. If the Aggressive Approach involves hiring new fundraising and marketing staff and the economy doesn't behave the way the leadership expects, the organization will be saddled with employees it may no longer be able to afford. Only under the Selective Approach, which counsels the slightest possible change in staffing levels, can the organization expect to face the future with the least possible disruption.

- The Selective Approach, in setting out a course between extremes, allows the greatest flexibility. For example, if you've ceased new-donor acquisition entirely, it may not be easy to start up again because that would require a large infusion of new cash—most of which could simply come instead from the proceeds of ongoing prospecting efforts under the Selective Approach. Similarly, if you've gone for broke in expanding donor acquisition, you may find that there's precious little cash available because the expanded program has sucked it all up in mailings that return only a small immediate return on investment.

Let's turn now, in the second part of this book, to a detailed look at the specific actions that could characterize an intelligent Selective Approach.

PART TWO

How You Can Face the Present More Calmly and the Future with Confidence

Anyone with more than a passing acquaintance with nonprofit management knows perfectly well that running a nonprofit is at least as complicated as running a business, and sometimes more so. The strategic response to adverse economic conditions such as those we face today must take shape in detailed plans that encompass hundreds of small decisions, ultimately involving everyone in the organization. In the ten chapters of Part Two, we'll explore nine principal recommendations that include many dozens of detailed suggestions stemming from the careful strategic response we arrived at in Part One.

CHAPTER 6

Reassess the Whole Ball of Wax
Fundraising, Marketing, Communications

You know the scene: for years, sailing's been smooth for your organization. But all of a sudden, somebody—a senior staff member, a trustee, or perhaps the executive director—notices that things aren't going quite so well. Net income's down sharply, or the rate of growth in the membership base has faltered, or major donors are starting to back away from their commitments. Or whatever.

It really didn't take a global financial meltdown and plummeting fundraising revenue to make *you* aware that your organization has a problem. You've known all along. But now other people are starting to realize that *something has to be done*.

It's already absolutely clear that you're not going to meet budget. Income simply isn't conforming to expectations. So without any prodding, you'll naturally rerun your financial projections for the season and the year. It's important that a budget be based on fact, not fiction. But that's hardly going to address the problem.

The board then meets, perhaps in an emergency session. Broadly speaking, it faces four alternatives when considering what to do about messaging, membership, and fundraising:

- Panic. Fire a whole lot of people. Turn the whole operation upside down. Maybe bring in a new executive director.
- Do nothing. Hope that the problem will go away on its own.
- Form a committee to study the problem to death.
- Recognize that resolute action is necessary, and charge the executive director with leading an immediate reassessment of the organization's fundraising, marketing, and communication activities from top to bottom, and recommending changes quickly.

As you've seen in Part One of this book, and as common sense would tell you anyway, three of these options make no sense at all—and that's true under any circumstances. Whether or not the problem has come to light because economic conditions are unfavorable, it's critical that the leaders recognize that a problem exists and get to the bottom of it without delay. Truth to tell, it's good practice to put in place a thoroughgoing management review from time to time even under the best of circumstances.

Before we explore the ways and means of a top-to-bottom review, let's confront an urgent and ugly question that comes up repeatedly in nonprofit leadership discussions when fundraising revenue drops off sharply: How do you decide between cutting fundraising, marketing, and communication expenses and cutting program activities?

What Do You Cut?

When you joined the organization, you never dreamed you'd face a dilemma like this.

Revenue from your fundraising program has fallen drastically, and you're under pressure from the executive director to slash donor acquisition costs. The only alternative, he says, is for him to cut program staff and thus serve fewer needy children. Every acquisition mailing represents a substantial net investment of cash. If you reduce your acquisition activities by 50 percent, that will conserve the necessary cash and permit the organization to keep all its program staff on board. How can you possibly question the executive director's demand when it's so clearly rooted in concern for the children you're all so committed to serving?

What can you say? How can you justify investing money in fundraising when so many more children are needy as a result of an economy in decline? How do you weigh the short-term needs for operating cash against the long-term need to ensure your organization's survival and thus its ability to serve children for many years to come?

I won't pretend there's an easy answer to this question. I can envision a nonprofit that offers survival services to poor people making the decision to do all it can in the short term and face the long-term consequences later, even if that might mean having to close its doors forever. Certainly some foundations adopt this attitude—and I applaud them. But for most nonprofit organizations, the trade-off between long-term and short-term needs is far more challenging.

If you're like the overwhelming majority of nonprofits, the vision that animates your work and the mission that gives it shape and direction recognize the long-term character of the issues you're confronting. Poverty, hunger, homelessness, disease, ignorance, oppression: none of these will respond to short-term solutions. I simply can't believe that even the most generously funded and skillfully managed effort can accomplish anything more than blunting the impact of these intractable challenges in the foreseeable future. Face it: if your organization is going to make a real difference in addressing real problems, you're going to need to be around for a long time to come.

You read in Chapter Four that a severe cutback in donor acquisition, even a temporary one, can shrink a donor base, reducing net fundraising revenue for years to come. So the question is whether you opt to continue prospecting for new donors or members—or spend the money instead to meet programmatic needs. In other words, when do you want your organization to suffer? Now or a few years down the road?

Framed in a more manageable way than a simple bipolar choice, the real question is this:

How can your organization maximize its programmatic impact in an era of growing demand and ever more limited resources while maintaining its ability to sustain its work for many years to come?

Viewed in this light, the resource allocation question is a little easier to discuss. For example, you could make the case that the organization will have to downsize in the future if it opts to cut back on new-donor acquisition in the near term—because the donor base will shrink to a greater or lesser degree, depending on the extent of the cutback. You might propose instead of a severe cutback that donor acquisition and other essential marketing and development activities be carefully monitored and their costs cut as judiciously as possible, thus freeing up some cash to support programmatic work (although not as much as cutting back acquisition by half).

It's your call—or your board's. In such challenging times, the only option you *don't* have is to ignore the question.

Now let's return to matters less fraught with ethical concerns: conducting a management review of your organization's fundraising, marketing, and communications activities.

Reassessing Your Work from the Outside In and the Inside Out

For starters, you may need outside counsel—a fundraising or marketing consultant. If that's beyond your means, especially in tough times, you might try to find a local volunteer skilled in evaluation or system design or a marketing professor from a nearby business school.

However, whether or not you engage a consultant, the management assessment you develop for your fundraising, marketing, and communications functions needs to reach far and deep into the organization's operations. It's important you use a method that forces you to take a dispassionate look at what you're doing—and evaluate *everything*.

One commonly used marketing evaluation tool, Ansoff's matrix, designed in the 1950s, helps to sort out the wheat from the chaff, but I find it less than user friendly. To give you a sense of why I'm not wild about attempting to shoehorn this tool into nonprofit planning, take a look at the general picture in Table 6.1.

A similar approach, the Boston matrix, developed by the Boston Consulting Group, does the job too, and I find it easier to explain and less troublesome to use.

TABLE 6.1 Ansoff's Matrix

	Existing Products	New Products
Existing Markets	Market penetration	Product development
New Markets	Market development	Diversification

Putting the Boston matrix to work requires that you sort each one of your fundraising, marketing, or communications "products" into one of four boxes or buckets, represented in a rectangle like that in Figure 6.1.

Here's how to allocate each of the four categories:

- *Dogs* are projects or programs that clearly aren't worth the time, effort, and money that go into them. They have low market share, and even if once upon a time they were growing quickly, that time has passed—for example, in a fundraising program, a high-maintenance house party program that's kept alive only because its defenders argue that the parties "create a lot of goodwill." Or an extensive program of online banner advertising that produces marginal results at best. Or a newsletter that's not demonstrably pulling its weight in donor satisfaction.

FIGURE 6.1 Boston Matrix

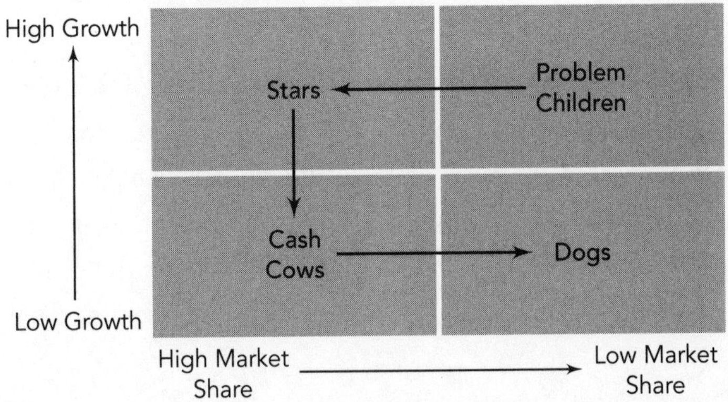

- *Cash Cows*, as the name implies, are programs or projects that generate a lot of net income but have little or no further growth potential—perhaps, for instance, an annual gala dinner that continues to bring in a significant share of the budget but has ceased to grow. Or a slick magazine that donor research makes clear is highly valued by the members but increasingly feels like a sinkhole for cash.

- *Stars* are programs with both high growth potential and high or increasing market share. In some nonprofits, legacy fundraising or major gifts, or even an online fundraising program, might fall into this category.

- *Problem Children* present something of a quandary, as you might imagine. They're growing or have clear growth potential, but they have low market share, perhaps because the staff hasn't quite gotten the hang of how to exploit their full potential. A face-to-face fundraising program ("direct dialogue") or direct mail program might be a Problem Child for a particular organization.

The working assumption (illustrated by the arrows that appear within Figure 6.1) is that over time, Problem Children that are successfully dealt with may gravitate from right to left and become Stars, Stars will sooner or later become Cash Cows, and eventually Cash Cows will become transformed into Dogs, with all their value sucked out of them.

It may be difficult to categorize all your fundraising, marketing, and communications programs in this fashion. Not everything will fit neatly into a little box. Some may come close to straddling a line between two categories. For example, a program that's growing but not generating any net revenue might be termed either a Dog or a Problem Child. In either case, if you were to plot each program at a precise point on the chart (rather than just lump them arbitrarily into one or another of the four buckets), a symbol representing that program could be put close to the line separating those Dogs and Problem Children, depending on your assessment of how its performance balances out. This might look something like the placement of the asterisk in Figures 6.2 or 6.3.

In this fashion, if you place each program carefully at a particular point on the matrix, you can represent the performance of your programs in a more balanced and realistic fashion.

Once you've reached agreement with your colleagues on the relative placement of each program, you'll be able to make more informed and dispassionate decisions about how to allocate your scarce available resources among the various programs. For example, you should consider the following:

- Eliminate all or most of the Dogs, keeping only those that are close to the line, either on top or on the left.
- Consider carefully whether you should also drop Problem Children. Their market share is low in a high-growth

FIGURE 6.2

FIGURE 6.3

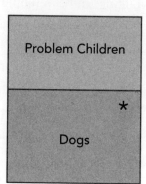

market, and it may take more than you can afford to build market share.

- Cash Cows cannot be cut—at least for the time being. Watch them closely, though, because sometimes there's only a thin line between a Cash Cow and a Dog.
- Stars deserve the most attention and the greatest share of available resources.

The objective of this exercise is to enable your organization to achieve a workable balance in your fundraising, marketing, and communications portfolio. Ideally you'll free yourself from the Dogs, and use some of the cash thrown off by your Cash Cows to turn Problem Children into Stars. If all you've got are programs that fit into one quadrant or another, that's a problem in its own right and will require you to invest in new initiatives that will bring some measure of equilibrium to your portfolio.

The Boston Matrix is neither a no-brainer to use (as you can see) nor trouble free. Here are a few of the warning signs to keep in mind as you apply this method to the reassessment of your fundraising, marketing, and communications efforts:

- The biggest problem with this approach is that, like so much else in the world of commerce and industry, it places a focus on short-term profits. In fundraising, many aspects of donor stewardship pay off over time by enhancing long-term donor value even if they bring in zero revenue in themselves. (In fact, the same might be said of customer relationship management in industry — a concept now much in vogue that's difficult to justify in terms of the quarterly bottom line.) It's advisable, therefore, to evaluate "profitability" or "productivity" in terms of long-term donor value. This will pose a challenge when it comes to brand building and other general marketing activities such as traditional image advertising. However, it shouldn't be all that difficult to distinguish between, say, a "friend-raising" special event that breaks even and a costly radio advertising campaign to build brand awareness.
- When the economy is in freefall, it's likely that most of your fundraising, marketing, and communications efforts

will start to look a little like Dogs. If performance is lagging in all areas, it may become far more challenging to make the choices the Boston matrix is designed to help you make.

- The assumption built in to the Boston matrix seems to be that every program must eventually get to be big if it's to be truly profitable. The method associates high market share with high profitability, which isn't always the case. Some highly profitable activities may work well only if they're conducted on a small scale. A high-dollar annual giving society, for example, might attract only a limited number of members but make a significant contribution both to the bottom line and to the growth of the major donor prospect pool.

- If fundraising or marketing programs were run by robots, this method would be a little easier to swallow. Regrettably, though, real people run nonprofit programs, and their jobs might be on the line. You'll need to take this into account, as any sensitive and effective manager would do, considering whether people might be easily shifted from one program to another, trained in new skills, or — if there's no alternative — whether they need to be helped to find jobs elsewhere. This is not to say that under no circumstances should anyone be fired or laid off. Sometimes that course of action is unavoidable. However, it's unwise and cruel to make such decisions without considering the human factor.

- Then there's the same problem with the Boston matrix that arises with any formulaic approach to planning: it necessarily oversimplifies. The Boston matrix is a useful evaluation tool, but it's no substitute for good, common-sense judgment.

Whether you use the Boston matrix or Ansoff's matrix—or somebody's proprietary method—isn't important. And it's not important whether you work with an outside individual or firm, or handle the whole thing in-house. What's critical is that you go through some systematic evaluation procedure designed to identify the strengths and weaknesses in your fundraising, marketing, and communications programs—and take decisive action to reallocate resources as necessary. This is good practice almost anytime. But it's essential when challenging economic conditions add pressure on your organization to conduct its affairs in the most cost-effective manner possible.

This assessment will spotlight the concrete actions you need to take to allocate resources: people, money, and time. But it won't address another vital element in the picture: messaging. That's the topic I take up in the following chapter.

CHAPTER 7

Strengthen Your Case for Giving

Tell me if I'm wrong about this.

You've been advised that it's essential you make clear to your donors how deeply the current recession has affected your organization. Your board of directors, your chief executive, your consultants—possibly even all three—are pressing you to talk about the recession in every fundraising letter, at every event, and to every major donor. The idea, of course, is that this will show your donors how much more valuable and important their contributions are during this difficult economic period—and, willy-nilly, they'll give more.

Would that it were so.

At this writing, I can't cite unequivocal and conclusive evidence that this is the wrong tack to take. However, a body of experience is accumulating that donors are more likely to be dissuaded from giving rather than induced to give more when you emphasize how heavily tough times are weighing on your organization. Clearly some donors are pre-disposed to dig more deeply when times are tough. They'll probably do so regardless of what you say about the impact of economic conditions on your organization and its work. Apparently, though, others are too easily reminded that (from their perspective, at least) times are tough for them too. And obviously it's not a great idea to scare them off.

Instead of taking this simplistic course, reconsider why your donors support you in the first place—and reexam-ine your case for giving in that light. What, after all, do your donors want from you?

- They want to know that you're doing the most effective job you possibly can with the money they give you.
- They want to know that their gifts are really reaching the people you're helping or affecting the issue you're addressing. (They're interested in impact, not in paying your salary or the office electric bill.)
- They want to know that you value their contributions.
- They want you to report the results of the projects and programs they've supported with their gifts.

All this is true regardless of economic circumstances. It's just a whole lot more important and urgent in difficult times, when any weakness in your organization can be multiplied many-fold by a donor public that's already skeptical to begin with and now may be financially strapped as well. However, if you act on the advice I offer in the chapters ahead, you'll be cutting costs and taking other steps to make your operation leaner. You'd be wise to communicate those steps to your donors. Write to them about how you're tightening your belt, increasing efficiency, and monitoring the productivity of your operations more closely. *Do not* talk about such problems as falling income from corporate and foundation grants and major gifts. Few donors really care about how you're hurting. They care about how well you're helping your clients or beneficiaries.

However, donor motivation normally runs much deeper than that. It starts with donors' affinity for your vision, mission, and values.

Vision, Mission, and Values

You've heard it before, no doubt: individual donors are far more likely to support your organization because of its vision, mission, and values than for any specific reason related to your work itself. If this is the case (and I certainly believe it is) and if your vision, mission, and values are unlikely to change with the seasons, then how can you strengthen your case for giving under difficult economic conditions?

Truth to tell, you can't—if, that is, you've done the best possible job of crafting a case for giving that relates directly to the core principles and values that animate your organization. Unfortunately, though, for a great many non-profit organizations, especially smaller ones, little thought, if any, has gone into what truly motivates people to give and what makes for a powerful case for giving.

So, for starters, what *is* a case for giving? (I just knew you were going to ask!)

In my view, there are two possible ways to interpret this familiar phrase:

- A case for giving is a copy platform or creative concept that is integrated into all fundraising and marketing materials produced by a nonprofit organization. It's a statement that positions the organization, describes how its vision takes shape in the real world, and lays out the benefits that a donor may receive for giving to the organization. A case for giving of this sort is generally no longer than a few sentences or a couple of paragraphs—one side of one sheet of paper at the most. It's not intended for external distribution.
- Alternatively, a case for giving may be a finished document that's either distributed with or integrated into a grant proposal to an institutional funder or a major individual donor. A document of this sort may run to many pages and be colorfully, even lavishly illustrated, printed, and packaged. Its sole purpose is to be handed (or, less frequently, mailed) to donors.

I've worked on both types of cases for giving. They're very different, as you can see.

The elaborate case for giving that a mature nonprofit might develop for a capital campaign or some other major fundraising program needs to include a number of items in detail:

- A statement of purpose that incorporates the vision, mission, and values of the organization
- A capsule history of the organization or a statement about the background of and need for the project or campaign
- The budget for the campaign, the project, or the organization as a whole
- A description of the sources of funds you anticipate, providing a context for the ask and assuring donors that you don't expect them to be the sole source of money for the project
- A time line for completion of the work
- A specific ask (or a range of asks)
- Information about donor benefits and recognition
- Illustrations, including charts, graphs, architectural drawings, and photographs, as necessary
- Especially in recessionary times, an explanation of how your organization will control costs and maximize return on investment

Each of these items might require a page or more to explain. It's not unusual for the case for giving in a major campaign to run twenty pages or more. Major individual and institutional donors are used to receiving pitches in this form. Apparently the stiff competition requires it.

But don't get the idea that writing the shorter case for giving is any easier. In fact, doing a top-notch job on any case for giving requires exploring donor motivation in some depth.

Why Donors Give (or Don't Give)

The motivation to give may be triggered by one or a combination of three components:

- **The emotional**—recognizing that not just impulse gifts but thoughtful, continuing support for a cause or institution may rest in large part on an emotional connection
- **The rational**—because few donors operate entirely in an emotional mode but must be convinced that a cause is credible and worthy of support on the basis of its vision, leadership, track record, or other factors
- **The spiritual**—reflecting the fact that much of philanthropy is rooted in spiritual values and beliefs, sometimes stemming from affiliations with organized religious bodies, sometimes more closely associated with deep-seated psychological impulses of the sort that psychologist Abraham Maslow categorized as self-actualization

Other than fundraisers for churches, synagogues, mosques, temples, and other religious organizations, most people in the field tend to overlook the spiritual dimension of donor motivation. Don't make that mistake. Many of your donors are likely to be supporting your work at least in part because you're helping to make the world a better place—by saving the world or preserving the planet, restoring human dignity, suppressing violence, or redressing injustice—and it's wise to keep reminding them of that broader contribution you're making. Others of your donors are no doubt motivated by overt religious beliefs, since research consistently shows that people who attend religious services regularly tend to be far more philanthropic than the average person. And whatever the roots of their motivation, the stresses imposed by a difficult economy may reinforce their inclination to give.

In a general sense, your case for giving must do the following:

- Describe how you will fulfill your mission and advance your vision if you receive the necessary funds
- Make clear how the gifts you receive will help you achieve the specific objectives of your campaign
- Emphasize in what ways, intangible and tangible, the donor will benefit from contributing to your cause or campaign

Viewed from a different perspective, your challenge in crafting a case for giving is to establish a link between your donors and your clients or beneficiaries or the issue you address. It's that connection you need to emphasize, not the connection between the donor and your organization itself.

Here are a few examples to make all this clearer.

Case for Giving for a Food Pantry

Your support for The Pantry will help bring closer the day when no one in our community will go to bed hungry at night. Your contributions of food and cash will demonstrate your commitment to sharing with those less fortunate than you and to building the caring community you want to live in.

Case for Giving for an Environmental Advocacy Organization

Save the Earth can win the case against global warming at all levels of government and throughout the business sector only with your active participation and generous support. In both ways, you help advance the media campaign and lobbying efforts that are central to our mission. Ultimately your unwavering commitment to leave our children and grandchildren a healthy, verdant planet and a sustainable economy will be the key to the survival of our way of life.

Case for Giving for a Community Orchestra

As a classical music lover, you know that the arts represent the finest expression of our civilization. Through your generous support for The Symphony, you help keep alive a centuries-old tradition of artistic excellence while making it possible for the young people of our community to express their innermost feelings and gain access to their talents through The Symphony's Music in the Schools program.

In practice, each of these cases might well be a little longer and more specific than I've indicated. Longer or shorter, though, the case for giving needs to connect with donors in every dimension of motivation—emotional, logical, and spiritual. And that language needs to be worked into every appeal and every communication with donors.

I recognize that many nonprofit organizations simply reprint their mission statements in newsletters and sometimes on appeals as well. I strongly believe that a case for giving along the lines I've described here will do a much more effective job of motivating donors.

To Ask or Not to Ask

Just as some folks in the nonprofit sector believe (wrongly, in my opinion) that it's a good idea to emphasize how tough times are when approaching donors, others believe it's important to postpone asking for money or, for an indeterminate period, stop altogether.

This is quite possibly the biggest fundraising mistake you could possibly make.

A decision to put off asking for money comes from the same impulse that makes many nonprofit folks apologize for asking. Never forget that a request for funds for your cause is an opportunity for your donors to validate their cherished values and beliefs. Ask! Your donors are grown-ups (presumably). If they can't give at this time, you'll find out soon enough. Chances are, though, many of them will be more offended if you *don't* ask than if you do.

Your donors *want* to support you. Don't get in the way.

Now join me in taking a look in Chapter Eight at whether it makes sense to try lots of new things when times are tough.

CHAPTER 8

Be Content with One in the Hand—Forget the Two That May Be in the Bush

ere's the part where my colleagues and competitors tell me to wash my mouth out with soap. (I know this, because several have already done so, although their language was a trifle less temperate.)

Now, nobody complains when I remark that this is not the time to move all the funds in your reserve accounts into one of those snazzy hedge funds that promises 25 percent annual returns. Or that it may not be wise to launch a capital campaign for a new office building when the old one is still functional. Certainly not in the middle of a global economic catastrophe.

No, the arguments come when I confront matters that cut a lot closer to the bone.

When you are facing the deadly combination of high or rising costs and an unhealthy economic environment that depresses response, there are at least two major factors to consider in deciding how much "creativity" to bring to bear in your fundraising program, especially when it comes to direct mail:

- First, there is the cost of testing—in time, complexity, and money. In flush times, when fundraising is healthy, the cost of direct mail testing is relatively inconsequential. An investment of a few hundred or a few thousand dollars in a sizable direct mail fundraising program might yield a substantial return on investment over time. That logic is harder to defend when resources are tightly constrained by a recession. My position is simple: *do less testing*. (There—I said it.)
- Second, there is the controversial question of the value of "creativity" itself. Admittedly, it's controversial only because I don't share the prevailing wisdom in fundraising that creativity is the key to success. My position on this question is simple too: despite what you may be hearing from experts, this is *not* the time for innovation. Creativity can be costly. *Stick with what works*. Be content with one bird in the hand, and don't go chasing the others that people tell you are out there in the bush.

Now, before you shut this book in disgust, please hear me out. I recognize that there may be little or nothing in your previous practice that's working now in this economy, so you may be forced to try new things. You may have no serviceable control package for your direct mail donor acquisition program. Perhaps none of your standard appeals—the ones you send, with slight variations, every year end, Easter, or Mother's Day—has been doing well during the past year. I don't mean to suggest you should eliminate all testing, in any event. Some high-priority tests are a good idea under any circumstances. And I don't recommend that you be uncreative. I merely suggest that you give careful thought to how creativity can be put to work in your fundraising program in a genuinely productive way and not simply as window dressing. So join me now as we take a look at each of these two topics in turn.

Good Tests Versus Inconsequential Ones

Consider a test that's in fairly common use by direct mail fundraisers: envelope color. In a very large-scale direct mail program, one we'll call Program A, there might be a statistically significant difference between the 0.64 percent return from a simple white outer envelope and the 0.66 percent from a kraft outer envelope that's otherwise identical. Over the long haul, an improvement in response of 0.02 percent could make a meaningful financial difference for Program A. But a difference of that order of magnitude is likely to be impossible to pin down for Program B, a mailer that employs small quantities in even the biggest of its mailings. In other words, that difference would likely be statistically *insignificant* for Program B. Unmeasurable, in other words. Under some circumstances, Program A should consider testing a white versus kraft carrier envelope. Program B should not, under almost any circumstance.

Now, lest you think I'm making this up out of whole cloth, I must tell you about an organization that tested this same concept year after year. In reviewing the results, I could almost never discern any difference in response that favored either the kraft or the white envelope. Clearly this test was worthless, but I was unable to stop the practice. Over time it must have cost the organization thousands of dollars to learn nothing useful. (The extra cost came from additional data-processing charges, extra costs in the letter shop where the appeals were packaged, and lower postal discounts on the smaller quantities available for each batch of identical packages.)

Or take another popular test that almost every direct mail fundraiser has employed, many of us time and time again: outer envelope teasers.

If you by any chance know who invented the teaser, and when, please let me know. If that person is still living, I'd like to give him or her a piece of my mind. No other innovation in direct mail fundraising (with the possible exception of the free sheet of address labels) has wreaked more havoc on later practitioners.

Is this hyperbole? You be the judge.

Over a period of several years, my agency, Mal Warwick Associates, tested "teaser versus no teaser" twenty-five times for nearly as many clients. We constructed what are known as A/B split tests, with half of a statistically significant selection of direct mail packages mailed in envelopes with a teaser and the other half mailed without one. Mailing quantities for each of the two variants were typically between 15,000 and 50,000 packages—big enough, under the conditions of each mailing, to obtain statistically valid results. Table 8.1 shows what transpired.

Does this experience suggest that it's wise to test teasers in your direct mail fundraising program these days, when money is so tight? Does it even suggest you should wrack your brain over possible teasers in the first place? Think about it.

I'll confess that I've long believed the ideal outer envelope for a direct mail fundraising appeal is one that is unmarked except for the sender's logo, name, and address; the addressee's laser-printed or ink-jetted name and address; and

TABLE 8.1 Testing Teaser Versus No Teaser

Version	Number	Percentage
Envelope with teaser won	1	4%
Envelope with no teaser won	3	12%
Neither version won	21	84%
Total	**25**	**100%**

postage, preferably either a live stamp or the imprint of a postage meter. Again and again I've seen envelopes like this return outstanding response rates and average gifts.

Are there exceptions? Of course! Anyone who's dogmatic about direct mail fundraising practices either hasn't been in the field for very long or is guided by stubbornness rather than logic and experience. I frequently use teasers in renewal notices, for example ("Your 2009 Renewal Enclosed" or "Last Chance to Renew for 2009"). Or when I think I've written a teaser for a donor acquisition package or a special appeal that seems as though it will be truly effective, I'll succumb.

In my 2003 book on testing for direct mail fundraisers, *Testing, Testing, 1, 2, 3*, I explain how to identify the types of tests that are most likely to bring to light significant differences:

- Acquisition lists (a must in any donor acquisition program).
- Whole new packages (as opposed to individual package components).
- Significantly different offers, including membership or donor benefits, involvement devices, front-end or back-end premiums, or ask amounts. (If you're unsure what I mean by using this jargon, you'll find explanations in any one of several of my books on direct mail fundraising.)

So at this point, you're either convinced or you're not. I won't press the case on testing any further. Instead I'll turn to the equally delicate topic of "creativity."

What's Really "Creative" in Direct Mail Fundraising?

Once upon a time in the Kingdom of Advertising, there were two brilliant and powerful princes who vied for supremacy in the realm. One was Bill, the Prince of Creativity. The other was David, otherwise known as the Prince of Benefits. For years, their battles seesawed back and forth across the land.

In modern times, we refer to these two princes of the art of advertising as William (or Bill) Bernbach (1911–1982), a cofounder of the legendary agency Doyle Dane Bernbach, and David Ogilvy (1911–1999), founder of the equally celebrated firm Ogilvy & Mather. Both agencies have been absorbed into the mega-agencies that typify this era of mergers and acquisitions, but the legacies of Bernbach and Ogilvy live on.

In their ongoing competition that gained iconic status for both of them, Bernbach would weigh in with extraordinarily creative contributions such as the advertisement in Figure 8.1.

Here is the copy you can't read in this low-resolution reproduction of Bernbach's ad:

> The Volkswagen missed the boat.
>   The chrome strip on the glove compartment is blemished and must be replaced.

FIGURE 8.1 Bill Bernbach ad for Volkswagen

Chances are you wouldn't have noticed it;
Inspector Kurt Kroner did.

There are 3,389 men of our Wolfsburg
factory with only one job; to inspect Volkswagens at each stage of production. (3,000 Volkswagens are produced daily; there are more
inspectors than cars.)

Every shock absorber is tested (spot
checking won't do), every windshield is
scanned. VWs have been rejected for surface
scratches barely visible to the eye.

Final inspection is really something!
VW inspectors run each car off the line onto
the Funktionsprüfstand (car test stand), tote up
189 check points, gun ahead to the automatic
brake stand and say "no" to one VW out of fifty.

This preoccupation with detail means
the VW lasts longer and requires less maintenance, by and large, than other cars. (It also
means a used VW depreciates less than any
other car.)

We pluck the lemons; you get the
plums.

Bernbach was a clever man, and his advertisements
attracted lots of attention and lots of laughs. They also sold a
lot of products, including the Volkswagens spotlighted in the
ad here. Creativity reigned in Bill Bernbach's domain.

Meanwhile, David Ogilvy scoffed at "creativity." He insisted that people didn't buy products because they thought the ads were funny or entertaining. They needed to be persuaded by facts—facts that brought to life the benefits they would receive from their purchases. One of Ogilvy's classic ads is illustrated in Figure 8.2.

Note the headline—one of the most famous in the history of advertising. Note too how much copy the ad contains. Ogilvy was a believer in the old saw that "long copy sells." (Who knows? Perhaps he even invented the phrase!) He was also a great lover of direct marketing, which Bernbach disdained, as most advertising people do to this very day.

Here's the full copy from that classic Rolls-Royce ad:

At 60 miles an hour the loudest noise in this new Rolls-Royce comes from the electric clock.

What *makes* Rolls-Royce the best car in the world? "There is really no magic about it— it is merely patient attention to detail," says an eminent Rolls-Royce engineer.

1. "At 60 miles an hour the loudest noise in this new Rolls-Royce comes from the electric clock" reports the Technical Editor of THE MOTOR. Three muffles tune out sound frequencies—acoustically.

2. Every Rolls-Royce engine is run for seven hours at full throttle before installation, and each car is test-driven for hundreds of miles over varying road surfaces.

FIGURE 8.2 David Ogilvy Ad for Rolls-Royce

The Rolls-Royce Silver Cloud—$13,995

"At 60 miles an hour the loudest noise in this new Rolls-Royce comes from the electric clock"

What <u>makes</u> Rolls-Royce the best car in the world? "There is really no magic about it— it is merely patient attention to detail," says an eminent Rolls-Royce engineer.

1. "At 60 miles an hour the loudest noise comes from the electric clock," reports the Technical Editor of THE MOTOR. Three mufflers tune out sound frequencies—acoustically.

2. Every Rolls-Royce engine is run for seven hours at full throttle before installation, and each car is test-driven for hundreds of miles over varying road surfaces.

3. The Rolls-Royce is designed as an *owner-driven* car. It is eighteen inches shorter than the largest domestic cars.

4. The car has power steering, power brakes and automatic gear-shift. It is very easy to drive and to park. No chauffeur required.

5. The finished car spends a week in the final test-shop, being fine-tuned. Here it is subjected to 98 separate ordeals. For example, the engineers use a *stethoscope* to listen for axle-whine.

6. The Rolls-Royce is guaranteed for *three years*. With a new network of dealers and parts-depots from Coast to Coast, service is no problem.

7. The Rolls-Royce radiator has never changed, except that when Sir Henry Royce died in 1933 the monogram RR was changed from red to black.

8. The coachwork is given five coats of primer paint, and hand rubbed between each coat, before *nine* coats of finishing paint go on.

9. By moving a switch on the steering column, you can adjust the shock-absorbers to suit road conditions.

10. A picnic table, veneered in French walnut, slides out from under the dash. Two more swing out behind the front seats.

11. You can get such optional extras as an Espresso coffee-making machine, a dictating machine, a bed, hot and cold water for washing, an electric razor or a telephone.

12. There are three separate systems of power brakes, two hydraulic and one mechanical. Damage to one will not affect the others. The Rolls-Royce is a very *safe* car—and also a very *lively* car. It cruises serenely at eighty-five. Top speed is in excess of 100 m.p.h.

13. The Bentley is made by Rolls-Royce. Except for the radiators, they are identical motor cars, manufactured by the same engineers in the same works. People who feel diffident about driving a Rolls-Royce can buy a Bentley.

PRICE. The Rolls-Royce illustrated in this advertisement—f.o.b. principal ports of entry—costs **$13,995**.

If you would like the rewarding experience of driving a Rolls-Royce or Bentley, write or telephone to one of the dealers listed on opposite page. Rolls-Royce Inc., 10 Rockefeller Plaza, New York 20, N. Y. CIrcle 5-1144.

3. The Rolls-Royce is designed as an owner-driven car. It is eighteen inches shorter than the largest domestic cars.

4. The car has power steering, power brakes, and automatic gear shift. It is very easy to drive and to park. No chauffeur required.

5. The finished car spends a week in the final rest shop, being fine tuned. Here it is subjected to 98 separate ordeals. For example, the engineers use a stethoscope to listen for axle-whine.

6. The Rolls-Royce is guaranteed for three years. With a new network of dealers and parts-depots from Coast to Coast, service is no problem.

7. The Rolls-Royce radiator has never changed, except that when Sir Henry Royce died in 193 the monogram RR was changed from red to black.

8. The coachwork is given five coats of primer paint, and hand rubbed between each coat, before nine coats of finishing paint go on.

9. By moving a switch on the steering column, you can adjust the shock-absorbers to suit road conditions.

10. A picnic table, veneered in French walnut, slides out from under the dash. Two more swing out behind the front seats.

11. You can get such optional extras as an espresso coffee-making machine, a dictating

machine, a bed, hot and cold water for washing, an electric razor or telephone.

12. There are three separate systems of power brakes, two hydraulic and one mechanical. Damage to one will not affect the others. The Rolls-Royce is a very safe car—and also a very lively car. It cruises serenely at eighty-five. Top speed is in excess of 100 m.p.h.

13. The Bentley is made by Rolls-Royce. Except for the radiators, they are identical motor cars, manufactured by the same engineers in the same works. People who feel diffident about driving a Rolls-Royce can buy a Bentley.

Price. The Rolls-Royce illustrated in this advertisement—f.o.b. principal ports of entry—costs $13,995.

If you would like the rewarding experience of driving a Rolls-Royce or Bentley, write or telephone to one of the dealers listed on opposite page.

Compare the copy in these two ads. The Bernbach promotion for Volkswagen is all about how terrific the car and the company that makes it are. It's a roundabout argument for the VW as a high-quality car. By contrast, the Ogilvy ad for Rolls-Royce dramatizes many of the genuine benefits of driving a Rolls: it's extremely quiet, easy to drive and park ("No chauffeur required"!), incredibly safe, and has available a variety of unique advantages, including hideaway picnic tables.

Bernbach's effort, while a classic in its own right, is what I call "manufacturer's copy." Ogilvy's copy is clearly designed to address a buyer's needs for information.

Are you wondering what all this has to do with the topic of this book? I thought so. Here, then, is why this enduring clash between the Bernbach and Ogilvy schools of advertising is so important—and so timely in today's chilling economic climate: a similar debate sputters on in the field of direct mail fundraising. On the whole, though—regrettably, so far as I'm concerned—it seems that Bill Bernbach won the contest.

Today, if my agency presents an appeal to a client that consists of a plain outer envelope containing a simple, straightforward letter, response device, and return envelope, it's a given that the client will complain that it's not "creative." No matter that decades of testing have proven to me beyond a shadow of doubt that most of what goes under the banner of creativity in direct mail fundraising today is counterproductive. If it's not colorful, attention getting, and clever—in other words, if it doesn't match up to the standards of Bill Bernbach—it's not "creative," and it won't fly.

Naturally it's not our clients alone who exhibit this attitude. All the trade associations where direct mail fundraising specialists congregate for conferences, workshops, and weekly luncheons celebrate "creative" packages in lavish, well-publicized award ceremonies. I know this firsthand, because my agency is winning lots of these awards nowadays.

Everybody loves awards, right?

In my not-so-humble opinion, the problem is that most of what goes into the creation of these "creative" packages is (a) expensive and (b) unnecessary. It's expensive because clever copywriters charge more money, top-flight designers have to create more elaborate and unusual packages, sometimes there are fees for photographs or other artwork used, and the printing costs are typically higher as well—sometimes much higher. A "creative" and colorful donor acquisition package can easily cost several thousand dollars extra to produce compared to a simple one that makes minimal use of color. In a mailing of, say, 100,000 packages, the added cost might amount to $25,000 or more.

Do these "creative" packages work? They certainly seem to. Some of the awards in direct mail fundraising are tied to results: poor results, no award. *But the question is whether a simple package could do as well, or almost as well, at a far lower cost—and thus be even more cost-effective.*

I believe the answer to that question is often yes. It's just not asked very often. Rarely are such elaborate packages tested against simple, straightforward, and inexpensive letter packages.

I suggest you start asking that question and doing the testing—especially now, when times are tough and you've got to make every penny count. Instead of striving for "creativity," set your sights on determining what works best. If that means you've got to roast another sacred cow, so be it.

CHAPTER 9

Cut Costs with a Scalpel, Not an Ax

If you're working for a nonprofit organization that hasn't recently undertaken an agency-wide cost-cutting program, you're clearly in a minority. Periodic cost cutting is simply good management practice. Cost cutting when money is tight is absolutely essential. And in the midst of an economic meltdown, it's inevitable.

The question, of course, is whether your efforts to cut costs will make for a leaner, meaner, and more productive organization—or damage staff morale and undermine rather than enhance your capacity to raise the funds you need to pursue your mission.

For example, I do *not* favor the percentage across-the-board staff cuts that are so popular when government agencies and corporations seek to lower their costs. I suspect that in a great many situations, the cost in lost productivity among those who remain is equal to or greater than the amount of money saved by the layoffs.

I won't address the usual sort of no-brainer cost-cutting measures, such as putting a lid on expense accounts and keeping tighter control of the office supplies. That sort of thing may or may not make sense for your organization. In any case, though, you've got lots of other places to turn for general cost-cutting recommendations of that sort. The steps I'll recommend are those that pertain specifically to fundraising. After careful thought, I've come up with sixteen cost-cutting recommendations. I'll round out the chapter with a box containing fourteen additional suggestions for cutting costs in print production.

1. Consider putting capital projects on hold.

Your accountant may advise you that the new office building you're planning to construct will be paid for with funds that have already been raised and from a different bucket than current operations, so the money you lay out for that project won't have any effect on your program work. If your capital reserves are sufficient and your balance sheet is strong enough, the accountant may be right. However, cash is cash, and in difficult economic times, your donors may want assurance that you're taking every possible opportunity to cut costs and restrict the outflow of cash. From a strategic perspective, it may make good sense to put that project on hold even though, from a financial perspective, it's not entirely necessary to do so. It's worth considering that step, obligations to your donors and other partners permitting.

2. Take a careful look at your organization chart.

Think about whether your organization needs to be flatter. For example, if your organization's staff is relatively small (say, fewer than thirty people in fundraising and marketing), it's possible you could function as well or better if you substituted a single vice president for fundraising and marketing for the three people now jockeying among themselves to set your course in both areas: directors of fundraising and marketing and vice presidents to oversee them both. A consolidation along these lines might bring added benefits by reducing compartmentalization and forcing resource sharing and coordination of efforts. With a smaller staff, of course, a change of that sort makes no sense, and with a larger one, it may well be impractical. But it's never a mistake to think about these things.

3. Make sure your fundraisers are actually raising money.

Be sure your major gift officers and legacy fundraisers are spending most of their time with donors or prospects, not flogging paperwork in the office. (If necessary, cut the paperwork requirements.) Many fundraisers have a pronounced aversion to actually raising money—and this represents a big cost. Some don't seem to like meeting with donors in the first place. Others enjoy the connections but manage to find excuses for not ever asking for money. (A colleague of mine blames the popular "moves management" process—an approach to major gift fundraising that emphasizes talking to donors but seems to drag out conversations—for this tendency.) You may be able to save the funds necessary to hire additional major gift and legacy fundraisers if you can find ways to ensure that your current staff is as productive as possible. No doubt, a move of this sort will be met by groans and complaints. But when times are tough, we've all got to pull our weight.

4. Rethink where you draw the line between major donors and small donors.

Many nonprofits—unfortunately, I believe—draw a hard line between the realm of major gifts and the work of the direct marketing or membership department. Most commonly, I've found, that line is drawn at the $1,000 level. Donors whose single gifts match or exceed that amount are automatically removed from the direct marketing people and relegated to the major giving staff, on the theory that personal attention will be more likely to elicit larger gifts from them.

There are three principal problems with this practice: (1) major gift officers are typically too busy (or think they are) to devote time to donors of such a modest amount as $1,000, and that often means those $1,000 donors receive no attention; (2) donors who have increased their support to the $1,000 level, often after many years of cultivation, have done so in response to direct marketing, not personal attention, and in many cases are uncomfortable about meeting in person or even, sometimes, by telephone; and (3) there is no reason whatsoever to believe that direct marketing (including communications by mail, telephone, and online) is unable to secure gifts above $1,000. In fact, my agency has been successfully soliciting gifts of $1,000 or more by what we call "high-dollar mail" for more than two decades. (You can learn about how we've done it in my book, *The Mercifully Brief, Real-World Guide to Raising $1,000 Gifts by Mail*.) Your organization may be able to save money on hiring major gift solicitors *and* increase net revenue by integrating high-dollar mail with your major giving efforts.

5. Reconsider that glossy magazine you send your donors.

Okay, it's true: sometimes a glossy magazine is an essential donor benefit, and eliminating it may jeopardize your organization's standing with its donors, including some major givers. However, after viewing such publications at dozens of nonprofits over the years, I've come to the conclusion that more often than not, these magazines cater to the staff's or the leadership's egos more than to the donors' desires. Enormous sums often go into the production and distribution of these magazines. Straightforward market research might demonstrate that the money is largely wasted. What I believe is more effective in reinforcing most donors' motivations to give are simpler, less expensive newsletters—so long as they cater directly to the donors, highlighting individuals or families who support the cause and reporting on the outcomes of donor-supported initiatives, rather than focusing on staff comings and goings. Coffee-table publications may be prestigious. But prestige doesn't pay the bills.

6. Consider outsourcing gift processing and donor file maintenance.

The hidden costs of an in-house back office are substantial: there are hiring, training, and supervisory costs, as well as space requirements, hardware, and software. You may be spending a lot more than you'd pay an outside service, but you won't know that unless you take into account all the costs of the operation. However, if you do decide to outsource the work, be sure to avoid bank caging (check processing) operations. I have yet to hear of a bank that has provided consistently good caging and cashiering service, and, sadly, I've heard horror stories about — well, you don't want to know. Instead, seek out a specialized firm that has an established track record of working with fundraisers. There are many scattered all over the United States and Canada and in a number of other countries as well.

7. Approach donor acquisition cautiously.

It's indisputable that response rates in direct mail donor acquisition have been falling, and the cost of recruiting donors has correspondingly risen for many nonprofits. However, the answer is not to slash the quantities of your donor acquisition mailings, much less to stop acquiring new donors entirely. (See Chapter Five, and especially, Figure 5.1, "Impact of a One-Year Lapse in Donor Acquisition," for an explanation of why this is such a bad idea.) Instead, you would be wise to analyze your donor file by calculating the long-term value of your donors by list of origin and favoring lists that have yielded donors with higher value. Admittedly, this practice is routine in many direct marketing programs. But those programs constitute a tiny minority of organizations heavily dependent on direct mail. And if you don't know how to determine long-term donor value, learn. (My book, *Revolution in the Mailbox, Revised Edition,* is one of a number of possible sources.)

8. Emphasize list exchanges in acquisition.

If you're renting outside lists extensively, you're paying a lot of money for the privilege. Sometimes this is unavoidable. You may find, for example, that some of your richest-yielding lists are available only on a rental basis. But those exceptions aside, when costs need to be minimized, it may make sense to give much higher priority in list selection to files that are available on exchange. The difference in costs can be $70 per thousand names or higher—or $700 for 10,000 names. If you rent, say, 50,000 names in a donor acquisition mailing, that could add $3,500 to the cost of the project, and $3,500 might represent the cost of acquiring 100 new donors or more.

Now, please don't tell me that your organization has a policy against exchanging names. In good times, when response to direct mail donor acquisition efforts is reasonably strong, you may be able to sustain that policy. Not when times are tough, though. This is one of those sacred cows you can't worship anymore. If necessary, go to your chief executive or the board. Do your best to make them understand that (a) nobody "owns" their donors, who undoubtedly give to many other nonprofits, *especially* to organizations that are engaged in similar work (your competitors), and (b) decades of experience in direct mail fundraising have made clear that an organization's direct mail program can be adversely affected by list exchanges only under the most exceptional circumstances—circumstances that are easy to avoid by setting limits in your arrangement with the supplier that will manage your list. If the powers that be counter that you've been promising a no-exchange policy for years, you can advocate asking permission from your donors to share their names as a way to lower your fundraising costs. The financial implications are significant.

9. Concentrate on reactivating lapsed donors.

For years, direct mail practitioners have realized that persuading donors who haven't given for a year or two to renew their support is normally both easier and cheaper than recruiting fresh new donors—and it has the added advantage that reactivated donors tend to be more responsive than newly acquired donors. If your organization has a sufficiently large list of lapsed donors (5,000 or more) so as to make a specially targeted mailing to them cost-effective, that's probably advisable. If you have telemarketing capacity within reach—either in-house or through an agency—that course may make even more sense. If the number of lapsed donors is too small or your capabilities are too limited, though, consider taking my approach in recommendation 10.

10. Mail long-lapsed and former donors in acquisition.
It's normal practice in direct mail to spend no more than three years at the outside to resolicit a donor. After that point, many mailers simply include the names and addresses of those who have failed to respond at all in a subsequent donor acquisition mailing. Such lists of former donors often prove to be highly productive, even rising to the top of the list ranking when the results are evaluated. And if a special lapsed-donor reactivation program is beyond your organization's means, you might consider including not just former donors (those who haven't contributed in thirty-seven months or more) but also lapsed donors (those who haven't given gifts for between eighteen and thirty-six months).

11. Make sure front-end premiums are cost-effective.
Those familiar front-end premiums—address labels, personalized notepads, bookmarks, calendars, greeting cards, and such—are regarded as a surefire way to boost response, especially in donor acquisition mailings, and there's a great deal

of truth to that. These near-ubiquitous "freemiums" probably account for the recruitment of the overwhelming majority of new direct mail donors. However, the jury's out on whether freemiums are a reliable way to enlist donors with long-term value to equal that of donors enrolled through straightforward donor appeals. (I know for a fact that in some cases they do not.) However, some mailers invest so much faith in front-end premiums that they may overlook their short-term as well as long-term costs. Quite apart from the cash flow implications—more expensive mailings drain cash more rapidly—the sheer cost-effectiveness of freemium mailings is worth a close look when money is tight. Be sure your direct mail program is optimizing the substantial investment you're making.

12. Gang-print your materials.

As you're well aware, printing in larger quantities brings economies of scale. The difference per piece between printing 10,000 brochures and 50,000 is substantial, and it's a lot more so when the difference is between 10,000 and 100,000 or 500,000. Obviously you're not going to save money merely by increasing the quantities of your print runs. However, there are at least three ways you might be able to do so: (1) ordering standard materials such as envelopes for a six- or twelve-month period rather than a single mailing; (2) finding ways to print several components of different mailing projects at one time; and (3) collaborating with noncompeting nonprofits in your area to print items of similar specifications together. (The charge for a "plate change"—a different layout or design using the same ink color or colors on the same size and shape of paper—can be negligible compared to the cost of printing the two items separately. By combining printed materials into a single print run, you can often save substantially.)

13. Clean your mailing list.

When you receive a piece of mail, where do your eyes first alight? Careful now. If you're like the overwhelming majority of people, what you notice first is your name and address. And if there's an error in addressing you, the chances are much greater that you'll toss the mail aside. Yet the state of "list hygiene" in the nonprofit sector is, on the whole, deplorable. Misspelled names, undeliverable addresses, missing zip codes, and dead people abound on many so-called donor lists. The owners of these lists are losing money two ways: wasting printing and postage costs on mail that goes nowhere but the trash, and discouraging or insulting donors. An intensive effort to clean your mailing list can significantly reduce the costs of mailing invitations to events, newsletters, and appeals. In the United States, the Postal Service maintains address changes that can be integrated into your mailing list through software that's widely available through service bureaus all over the country. It's always worthwhile updating your list at least annually—if not with every large mailing you send. If your list is relatively small, it's worth the time to edit it, line by line, to correct obvious errors.

14. Reduce your postage expenses.

Commingle. It sounds almost obscene. But according to my colleague Brienne Collison, a production wizard from the word go, it's the key to reducing postage costs. As Bri explains, commingling is the process of merging several portions of a mailing that might otherwise go out independently into a single mail stream, permitting the mailer to realize higher discounts. This is the case because the process effectively performs some of the work that the U.S. Postal Service would otherwise have to do itself. It enables the mailer to skip several steps in the distribution of the mail, shipping directly from the mail shop (or letter shop) to a special commingling facility—and thence directly to the regional mail centers closest to the points of delivery. Commingling has the added advantage of shaving the time that lapses from the letter shop to home delivery—an average of more than two days with nonprofit bulk rate mail. (There's a lesser bonus as well: with commingling, mail that must travel farther is processed first, helping to even out delivery dates to a more uniform pattern.) Given that the process was developed by the post office, there are restrictions and requirements galore, but none that an alert and professional letter shop can't deal with. And here's the kicker: *small mailings benefit the most.* The savings are greatest with mailings of between 20,000 and 200,000 pieces. For example, in a mailing of 20,000 letters, the savings may approach $700.

15. Trim telemarketing costs.

Because telemarketing is an expensive way to communicate with donors, names selected for inclusion in any given project are often carefully limited. However, there may be a little room for reducing costs by limiting the quantity further. There are at least three ways to do this: (1) ensuring that donors who have previously declined to give by phone are eliminated from the project; (2) limiting quantity further, calling only donors who have previously given by phone; and (3) raising the minimum gift level of the names you'll call. In truth, any or all of these practices may be advisable even when you're flush. After all, what's the point of wasting money?

16. Scrutinize online communications costs.

The cost structure of online fundraising is different from that of direct mail or phone fundraising, because once you've set up your system, the cost to send each additional message, or to personalize or segment messages, is negligible apart from staff time. But there are still ways to waste money online. For example, if you're spending a lot on banner advertising, which is seldom effective for nonprofits, consider spending that money on Google keywords, especially if you can't get a Google Grant for free keywords. (If you're unfamiliar with Google Grants, Google the term!) While you can spend hundreds of thousands of dollars—and almost as many hours—creating a new Web site, think carefully about what you really need and what will really work, and invest the extra money in building a larger list of e-mail subscribers, activists, and donors. If you're spending tens of thousands of dollars to create videos for YouTube, consider a quick-and-dirty style that often works as well or better for short Web videos. If you have a very large e-mail list, but 20 or 30 percent of the people on it haven't opened a message in a year or more, you may want to archive those names and save some money if you are paying your provider based on the number of records in the e-mail database.

•••

There you have it. If you can't find something that works for your organization among those sixteen cost-cutting recommendations—or among the additional fourteen ideas in Dan Suzio's box that follows—then my hat's off to you. (Maybe you should teach *me* how to cut costs?) Perhaps instead you'll find recommendations more relevant to your fundraising program in the following chapter, which takes up the vital question of segmentation.

Fourteen Ways to Cut Design and Production Costs
Dan Suzio

My former colleague, Dan Suzio, who was for many years my firm's production manager, once wrote that "if you really want to know how to cut your direct mail design and production costs while increasing response, my best advice is to work as a printer for a few years." Since you probably can't do that, I'll pass along some of Dan's favorite tips (as updated by Brienne Collison).

• • •

1. Get to know your printers as well as you can. Take a tour of the shop, and meet the press operators and prepress technicians. Ask lots of questions. Show them samples and sketches, and ask what you can change to make their job easier or faster (and therefore cheaper). If your printer isn't willing to help, find one who is.

2. Be available when the printer calls with a question. You don't want your job to get bumped from the press because you were too busy to take the call. And you especially don't want someone else to decide what you really mean when your instructions are unclear.

3. Learn printing jargon. You might not need to know the difference between "work and turn" and "work and tumble,"

but you should know the difference between a monarch envelope and a #7–3/4 (they're the same size, but there is a potentially expensive difference).

4. Know what various kinds of presses can and can't do. You should know the quality and cost differences between sheet-fed printing, open web, heat-set web printing, jet off-set, flexographic, and any other kinds of printing that you encounter. You can often get surprisingly good quality with some of the so-called low-end printing processes. A good printer will be willing to experiment with screens, halftones, bleeds, and so on to get the results you want.

5. Know when to ask for PDF proofs, color proofs, and press checks, and what to do with them. Don't waste time and money on a press check, or even a color proof, when you don't need one. I don't have any set rule to give you, but in direct mail fundraising, PDF proofs are almost always good enough. (And make sure you've done your proofreading *before* the job goes to the printer. Making copy changes or corrections at the proof stage is a waste of the printer's time and your money.)

6. Design a size that makes sense in terms of press size, paper size, personalization, and letter shop. Standard sizes are standard for a lot of reasons, not least of which is cost. For example, an 8.5" × 11" letter fits twice on an 11" × 17" plate, or four times on a 17" × 22" plate, but if you make it a half-inch bigger—say, 9" × 11" or 8.5" × 11.5"—it will fit only once on the smaller plate, or twice on the larger one, doubling the press time and increasing the paper cost. (If

you want a piece to stand out and still be affordable, make it smaller, not bigger.)

7. When using laser personalization, how many pieces can you fit on a sheet? (It depends on your vendor's equipment.) Lasering two-up saves up to 50 percent. For larger quantities, look into continuous-form laser printing—but don't forget to add the extra cost of printing and bursting continuous forms.

8. Make sure all of the pieces fit into the outer envelope, with enough room to spare to allow machine inserting. Use photocopies to make a sample before it's printed, and ask your letter shop about the size and clearance requirements of its inserting equipment. (And make sure the response device fits into the reply envelope.)

9. If you design something with a bleed—that is, the ink goes all the way to the edge of the paper—it has to be printed oversize and trimmed. You may want to make the finished size smaller; ask your printer how much extra paper will be used by the bleed. Better yet, don't bleed any images off the page. Bleeds rarely add any value to a direct mail package. They just make designers happier.

10. Printing a three-color job requires two passes through a two-color press or using a more expensive four-color press. Either way, that third color is going to cost you. For a cheaper alternative, use screens or overprints to make a third color with only two colors of ink. To see what screens and overprints will look like, check with a graphic arts supply company for the various color guides published by Pantone.

11. Some folds cost more than others; some are possible only by hand. Use your imagination, but be sure to ask what it will cost.

12. Keep samples of everything you print, and label them with the weight of the paper. Use them to make weight samples; if your package is going to be overweight, you want to do something about it before it goes to the printer. Remember that paper can absorb moisture, which adds to its weight. If you've designed a first-class mailing that's over 0.95 ounces, you should probably trim something. Otherwise you could get an expensive surprise when it reaches the post office.

13. Put it in writing. Your purchase order should specify all of the printing specs, delivery date and place, quoted price, maximum overs and unders, type of proofs needed, number of samples needed, and anything else you can think of.

14. Mechanical artwork should have a tissue overlay showing all color breaks, screens, bleeds, and so forth. Art files should always note any folds, perforations, and scores. If you send art to your printer by e-mail or FTP, also e-mail or FTP PDFs of the finished components. If an art file is too large to e-mail or FTP to your printer, send the art on a disk accompanied by a laser proof PDF of the final component. Folds, perforations, and scores should also be indicated. Never leave anything to the printer's imagination.

CHAPTER 10

Fish Where the Big Fish Are

How many donors does your organization have?

Think carefully now. Don't make the mistake so many of my clients have made over the years when they began work with my agency and simply recite the total number of people on your "mailing list." More often than I can possibly recall, a client has told me its list numbers 25,000 or 50,000, though a simple subsequent analysis showed that no more than 3,000 or 5,000 of the people on the file could honestly be called "donors." Nonprofit mailing lists all too often contain hundreds or thousands of names that were added (and never removed) because they signed up for a free newsletter, or someone in-house thought they ought to be interested in the organization's work, or they stopped by the office to express interest, or they attended an event in 1989 but have done nothing since.

With few exceptions, all of these added names are deadwood. (They may have value as warm prospects, but you're wasting money on continuing efforts to solicit them or invite them to events when they've clearly demonstrated an unwillingness to respond.) The first job of the process of segmentation is to identify them and allow you to stop wasting money by including them in your fundraising appeals. This is one of the most dramatic ways a nonprofit organization may be able to cut its fundraising costs.

Segmentation is especially valuable when times are tough. First, segmentation can increase your net revenue by limiting your solicitations to the most productive donors. Second, if it is conducted correctly, it will help keep your best donors active, which can help make up for cuts in new-donor acquisition.

How Segmentation Works

Let's say your mailing list contains 20,000 names with postal addresses. You're planning your fundraising schedule for the year ahead, and for budgetary reasons alone you need to determine how many people will be included in each of the several appeals you're contemplating. So let's get started with a simple segmentation of your 20,000-name file.

There are four fundamental criteria to take into consideration in a simple segmentation:

- **Recency**—the date on which you received the most recent contribution from a given donor. In general, donors who have given most recently are the most likely to respond to a current appeal. (Yes, even though logic may tell you that someone who just gave is unlikely to do so again very soon. Experience shows that's not the case.)

- **Frequency**—the number of times a donor has contributed to your organization, usually within a given period of time (the most recent two years, for example). Typically a donor who has given frequently in recent times is highly likely to give again when you ask.

- **Giving level**—the amount of money you received from a donor. Giving level may be defined as the largest gift ever; the largest gift received during, say, the past two years; or the cumulative amount of money the donor has given you over a lifetime or during the most recent two years (or some other standard period). With the possible exception of donors acquired through front-end premium mailings, a donor of larger gifts will probably be more responsive to your next appeal than one whose gifts have been smaller—all other things being equal (namely recency, frequency, and source).

- **Source**—the channel through which a donor's first contribution was received—whether direct mail, special events, face-to-face ("direct dialogue"), television, telemarketing, online, or something else. The rule of thumb in fundraising is that it's easiest to secure a second gift

from a donor by soliciting her through the same channel her first gift came through. For example, direct
mail–acquired donors are far more likely to respond to
a new direct mail appeal than special event–acquired
donors are.

This process will enable us to locate "where the big
fish are" so we don't go fishing for contributions without a
pole or bait.

Let's now explore that 20,000-name list of yours using
these four criteria.

First, we may find that only 10,000 of the 20,000 people on your list have ever given gifts to your organization. We
may also learn that 3,000 of those 10,000 donors haven't given
a dime in more than three years, and an additional 2,000
haven't given during the past twenty-four months. Thus, using
a broad definition of an active donor—one who has contributed at least once during the most recent twenty-four
months—your donor list in fact consists of 5,000 people, not
20,000.

Now, of those 5,000 people, we may discover that
1,000 have given during the past six months, 1,000 during the
preceding six months, and 3,000 gave last year but not this year.
Table 10.1 shows the recency distribution in tabular form.

We may also learn that 300 of the 5,000 people have
each given five gifts or more during the past twenty-four
months, 300 have given four gifts during that time, 400 have

TABLE 10.1 Distribution of 20,000 Names by Recency

Recency of Last Gift	Number of Donors
0 to 6 months	1,000
7 to 12 months	1,000
13 to 24 months	3,000
25 to 36 months	2,000
37 or more months	3,000
Never	10,000
Total	**20,000**

contributed three times, and 3,000 have given twice. The other 6,000 people have given only once during the past two years. Table 10.2 restates these numbers in a table.

Now for a look at giving levels. We'll use the highest previous contribution (HPC) to determine the level of giving, because that's the most commonly used formulation in direct mail fundraising. Analysis shows that 6,000 of the

TABLE 10.2 Distribution of 20,000 Names by Frequency

Frequency of Giving*	Number of Donors
5 or more gifts	300
4 gifts	300
3 gifts	400
2 gifts	3,000
1 gift (reactivated)	1,000
1 gift (new)	5,000
0 gifts	10,000
Total	**20,000**

*During the most recent twenty-four months.

20,000 people on your list have given gifts of between $1 and $25 on at least one occasion. Another 3,000 gave between $26 and $100. A total of 1,000 others gave at least one gift each of $101 or more: 700 from $101 to $500, 295 from $501 to $1,000, and just 5 greater than $1,000. These numbers are set out in Table 10.3.

For the sake of argument, let's assume that all 10,000 of the actual donors were acquired by direct mail, so we don't need to take the source into account. Now all we have to do is combine the 1,000 people who contributed at least once during the past six months, the 300 people who have given five or more gifts, and the five donors who have given at least one contribution of $1,000 or more, find out which ones fall into all three groups, and—voilà—we'll know who our best donors are, right?

Well, not exactly. As, of course, you've already figured out for yourself.

TABLE 10.3 Distribution of 20,000 Names by Giving Level

HPC*	Number of Donors
$1,000 or more	5
$501 to $1,000	295
$101 to $500	700
$26 to $100	3,000
$1 to $25	6,000
$0	10,000
Total	**20,000**

*During the most recent twenty-four months.

Chances are, in fact, that there are exactly zero donors who fit into all three top categories, or segments. Donors of $1,000 gifts are not normally prone to give five or more times in the course of two years. In the real world, we need to rely on computers to crunch the numbers for us and identify the "best" donors by weighing all three criteria at once: recency, frequency, and giving level. By giving equal weight to all three criteria, a properly programmed computer can produce a simple segmentation plan such as the one shown in Table 10.4.

In Table 10.4, segment 1, characterized as high-dollar donors, contains individuals who have contributed at least one gift of $250 or more during the past thirty-six months. By contrast, segment 2, core active donors, consists of those who have given at least one gift of $50 or more during the past eighteen months but have given at least two gifts during that period—excluding those who fall into segment 1. By this process of elimination, you can categorize donors as segments 3, 4, and 5 in a similar manner.

A word of caution, however: don't treat these guidelines as gospel. Determine your own categories by analyzing the behavior of your own donors. You may discover that the giving levels used here don't work for your organization.

By using these hypothetical standards, this process might result in a distribution of the 20,000 names in our example like that in Table 10.5.

TABLE 10.4 A Simple Segmentation Plan

Segment	Label	Recency	Frequency of Gifts*	Giving Level*
1	High-dollar donors	0–36 months	1 or more	$250 or more
2	Core active donors	0–18 months	2 or more	$50 or more
3	Noncore active donors	0–18 months	1 or more	$25 or more
4	Lapsed donors	19–36 months	1 or more	$1 or more
5	Former donors	37 or more months	1 or more	$1 or more

*During the most recent twenty-four months.

TABLE 10.5 Distribution of 20,000 Names by Segment

Segment	Label	Number of Donors
1	High-dollar donors	300
2	Core active donors	1,700
3	Noncore active donors	3,000
4	Lapsed donors	2,000
5	Former donors	3,000
	Nondonors	10,000

In this ultimately simple and straightforward fashion, we've identified the 5,000 active donors out of a total of 20,000 people on a mailing list and broken down those 5,000 names into three categories: 300 of the very "best" donors; 1,700 who are both generous and responsive; and 3,000 who are active and still ought to be considered good prospects for additional support under most circumstances. With this information under your belt, you're prepared to make more intelligent choices about whom to include in an upcoming direct mail appeal—and whom to exclude.

For example, if your priority is to maximize net income from an appeal, you might elect to mail to only those 5,000 people—or even just the 2,000 people in segments 1 and 2. You'll save a bundle on production and mailing costs if you don't mail to the other 15,000 or 18,000 people on the list—and you'll be appealing just to donors who appear to be most disposed to give again.

That's what I mean by fishing where the big fish are.

But there's a lot more to segmentation that can further increase your net revenue.

How Segmentation Can Boost Your Bottom Line

There are four basic ways you can maximize your net income through segmentation:

1. Save money by not mailing—or phoning, visiting, or inviting to special events—anyone who has failed to respond to appeals during the past three years (or two years, or one)—unless, of course, their giving levels are high enough. A $1,000 donor from three years ago might well be worth another shot.
2. Save even more money by appealing only to donors who fall into one of your top-most segments.
3. Increase net revenue by investing more in the donors in your top one or two segments through personalization, higher production values in mail or longer times on the phone, or combining e-mail in advance and follow-up by phone with an appeal to these best donors.
4. Increase net revenue by creating different versions of an appeal, based on significant differences in behavior among your donors. For example, a Jewish charity might send an appeal for assistance to Israel to donors who have previously responded to pro-Israel appeals and one about domestic concerns to donors who have not responded to

appeals about Israel. (This variable—having given to sim-ilar appeals in the past—can often trump recency, fre-quency, and giving level as a predictor of response.)

Perhaps your usual practice is to mail appeals to all your donors by nonprofit bulk mail. After culling the donor list of any deadwood, you might now carve out, say, the top 10 percent or top 200 individuals and invest in truly person-alized appeals to them, embedding multiple data points from your database in each individual letter. Refer to such matters as the number of years a donor has been contributing to your organization; whether she has pledged to leave a legacy gift; whether she is a volunteer, an event attendee, a monthly donor, a retiree—in short, any significant matter that helps set one donor apart from others. Appeals that are truly per-sonalized in this fashion have been proven to yield much higher rates of response.

This discussion leads us smoothly into the subject of Chapter Eleven: getting closer to your donors.

CHAPTER 11

Stay Close to Your Donors

You've heard it a thousand times: fundraising isn't really about money—it's about *relationships* with donors. But does your organization have programs in place that truly reflect this perspective? If your approach is like hundreds of others I've observed firsthand, probably not.

In your major gift program, for example, the byword is *bonding*. Yet how many hours per week do your major gift officers spend meeting face-to-face with donors and prospects? How many of your board members or senior managers are personally acquainted with your top donors? In what ways do you keep your biggest donors up to date on the principal programs and issues that affect your work? If you have good answers to these questions, go to the head of the class. You're not alone—but the space up there isn't crowded.

Now, when money is tight, you can't worry just about your major givers. It's doubly important that you operate as though all your donors are your best friends in the world. (In more ways than one, they are.) To survive tough times and thrive when the economic storm clouds lighten, you need to devote a great deal of attention to thinking about how you can make your donors' experience with your organization more meaningful.

In recent years, there has been an increasing amount of research into donor motivation by both practitioners and academics. As a profession, we fundraisers have begun to learn a lot about what moves donors and what doesn't. Researchers have plumbed the depths of a hundred questions or more. But one fact does seem to emerge clearly from almost all of what I've read: donors crave appreciation for their gifts—and they're likely to become downright cranky if they're not thanked promptly and warmly.

No doubt you're attentive to the need for acknowledging major gifts. But how about gifts in smaller denominations?

In direct mail circles, many fundraisers lament the low rates of conversion from one-time to multiple givers, and the higher but still sobering rates of renewal of multiyear donors. Yet many direct mail fundraising programs skimp on—or entirely avoid—donor acknowledgments. I know this is the case, because for a great many years, I conducted an annual test of thank-you practices by major American mailers (what's called "mystery shopping" in other countries). I was truly appalled by how many sent gift acknowledgments only weeks or even months after the fact—or failed to send any at all. I'm certain, without any doubt whatsoever, that the poor renewal rates that plague so many direct mail fundraising programs are partly the result of this cavalier treatment.

What do donors want the most? They want to be treated as human beings, not statistics. Yet is this the message you deliver when you mail generic thank-you notes by bulk mail, when donors receive them weeks after sending their gifts, when all they get after giving online is an instant e-mail acknowledgment with no follow-up, when your gift acknowledgments include not a hint of the appeal that gave rise to the donors' gifts, or when (to make matters even worse) your thank-you is a postcard rather than a letter?

Sure, times are tough. Your budget has been cut, and cut some more. Yet this is *not* the time to economize on gift acknowledgments. In fact, to gain a sorely needed competitive advantage in this era of tight money, you would be well advised to spend more, not less, on expressing appreciation to your donors.

If you're laughing now—or groaning; the difference is immaterial—I suggest you consider taking another look at the preceding chapter on segmentation. Spending *more* on gift acknowledgments to a *smaller* number of donors can still save you money. Think about it.

Give Your Donors That Warm and Fuzzy Feeling

Prompt, personalized thank-you notes won't do the trick alone. It's important that your donors—especially your most generous and responsive donors—get the feeling that you care about them more than just as sources of cold, hard cash. This is the impression they're likely to get if you:

- Never communicate with your donors except to ask for money.
- Ask for an additional gift as soon as you receive the last one.
- Include a postage-paid reply envelope with every gift acknowledgment.

I'm well aware that many direct marketing specialists heartily recommend such practices. I think they're wrong.

Three decades ago when I began my career in fundraising, it made perfectly good sense to undertake a consistently aggressive solicitation program. Competition, at least by today's standards, was slight. Most direct marketing donors were less sophisticated and less demanding. But times have changed, and so have donor attitudes.

Today donors demand heartfelt appreciation, considerate and responsive treatment, and information that inspires their trust. It's not enough to ask them for money. You'll need to keep them well informed about your organization's work in general and about the specific projects and programs they've supported.

Here are ten low-cost ways you can build cultivation efforts into your fundraising program:

1. Call your best donors and thank them personally, making it very clear that you're not asking for more money—you're thanking them.
2. Make sure that the signature on your communications with your top donors is that of the chief executive or chair of the board. If possible, arrange for them to sign letters personally.
3. Develop an insider's newsletter in the form of a chatty, occasional letter from your CEO or executive director, mailed exclusively to your best donors.
4. Send selected donors a white paper or special report with a personalized cover letter and a card from the chief executive or a specific program person, soliciting questions and comments. Such a report needn't be written especially for donors. Chances are you'll have at hand a variety of reports, analyses, and memoranda from your program staff. Surely there's something that can be easily adapted.
5. When a favorable story about your organization or the issue you're addressing appears in print, send a tearsheet or a photocopy to each of your donors with a small note affixed ("In case you missed this . . .").

6. For your very best donors, send an autographed copy of a book written by a staff member about an issue related to your organization's work. Include the executive director's business card and a handwritten thank-you note.

7. Organize an open house at your headquarters, field office, or service facility, and invite all your donors. Relatively few are likely to attend, but they'll all appreciate the invitation.

8. Establish a free twice- or three-times-annual conference call on timely subjects, with the executive director or a senior program director conducting a twenty-minute briefing followed by forty minutes of questions and discussions. Invite all your donors if their total number is small. Limit it to the top segment or segments if the number is likely to be unwieldy.

9. Organize an intimate program briefing for top donors and board members only, giving your donors a feeling of inclusion in the leadership.

10. Organize a tour of your projects overseas, in distant areas of your country, or simply in your facilities, inviting top donors to participate at their own expense (if any).

With a little imagination, you can almost certainly come up with other ideas specifically tied to your organization's mission and programs. With a little cash as well, you can do even more with technology.

Use Technology to Get Closer to Your Donors

Careful now. When you saw the word *technology*, did you think of e-mail, the Internet, social networks, and text messaging?

These latter-day communications technologies have many productive uses, but I believe the most effective tool to use in closing the gap between your organization and your donors is the telephone. And its value increases in times like these, with economic pressures on us all and a widespread tendency among fundraisers to lessen contact with their donors out of fear of scaring them off.

Telemarketing gets a bad rap among most fundraisers. In part, this is because most of us (yes, even I) become unhinged when our dinners are interrupted by telephone solicitors, especially when the call is coming on behalf of organizations we've never heard of and have no intention of supporting. In part, too, it's the legacy of the early days of telephone fundraising, when so many early entrants in the field instructed their (ill-informed) operators to read verbatim from formal scripts. And our attitudes about telemarketing aren't helped in the least by all the negative publicity about telephone scams and greedy telemarketers.

Despite the drawbacks, telefundraising, a professional variant on telemarketing, has helped American nonprofit organizations raise tens of billions of dollars while informing donors and cultivating stronger long-term relationships with them. During the two decades I was involved in telefundraising as a principal of a company in the industry, I can honestly say that my company received more reports from clients about favorable comments from donors than we did about complaints.

To give you some idea of the power of the telephone to stimulate giving, consider this: repeated assessments by my telefundraising company revealed that donors who'd said no on the phone were significantly more likely to respond to a subsequent direct mail appeal than donors who had never been reached. (Yes, they'd said no, but they gave later through another channel.)

Why does the telephone work so well? It's simple. With a trained and well-informed caller, the interactivity of telephone contact offers an ideal opportunity to craft your case for giving in terms that respond directly to the values and priorities of individual donors.

Here are just seven of the many ways you can use the phone to get closer to your donors:

1. Join with your major giving and legacy giving officers in calling all the donors and prospects served by those two departments. Explain to all your donors and major prospects exactly how you're coping with the economic crisis: what new efforts you've undertaken to assist your clients or beneficiaries, what steps you've taken to economize, and how much you value the support from the public that enables you to continue your important work

even during these difficult times. *Do not* ask for money on the call.

2. Organize a "thank-a-thon" for staff and volunteers to call all your donors (or all the active ones, or the best ones) simply to express appreciation for their contributions—not to ask for more money. This can be a lot of fun, reinforcing the good feeling of donors and volunteers alike.

3. Recruit board members to make thank-you calls to donors of significant gifts, assigning each board member a small number of calls per month. Although many board members are reluctant to take on this responsibility, some will—and their reports about how rewarding it was may prove infectious. Like a thank-a-thon, this practice can serve as an excellent motivator for board members as well as donors.

4. Phone every new donor shortly after receiving the donor's first gift simply to express appreciation—not to request more money. For a larger organization that must use a professional telefundraising company to make the calls, this is admittedly an expensive proposition. But if funds permit, it can result in significantly higher first-year renewal rates, thus lowering future donor acquisition costs. In a smaller organization, you might assign this task to a volunteer who will make the calls from home. (One prominent Catholic charity gave the task to retired nuns.)

The minimal investment in the calls themselves will yield big dividends in added donor loyalty.

5. Phone lapsed donors who have failed to respond to several direct mail renewal efforts to persuade them to continue giving. Telephone reactivation has consistently proven to be more effective than reactivation by mail. So even if you're forced to pay dearly for an agency to make these calls, you'll almost certainly find that the cost of "reacquiring" those donors is less than the cost of replacing them with new, first-time donors. You'll also find that reactivated donors are likely to be more responsive than first-time donors. And if you're successful in reactivating lapsed donors, you might try phoning long-lapsed or former donors. (In doing so, it's prudent to begin with, say, thirty-seven- to forty-eight-month lapsed donors, and, if successful, testing forty-nine- to sixty-month lapses.)

6. Phone your donors at random simply to say thank-you and to ask a few standard questions. I'm not familiar with any efforts to do this using a professional telefundraising agency, but on several occasions I've succeeded in persuading development staff members of my clients to stay late into the evening and make such calls at random. It's best, I believe, to ask no more than three or four questions. (You might consider asking, for example, whether the donor has any questions or comments about the organization; why the donor supports you; whether you represent a philanthropic priority for the donor or are just

one of many nonprofits she supports; or whether she will allow you to use her name and a brief comment in support of the organization and its work on your Web site or in printed materials.) Typically the staff members who try this out find that it can become addictive: these conversations are heartening as well as revealing—and they're an ideal way to boost donor loyalty. Naturally you can determine the selection of donors to call using any one of a limitless number of segmentation criteria.

7. Use the phone to persuade frequent donors to become monthly supporters. Almost universally, direct marketing fundraisers find that the telephone is far more effective in converting one-off donors to monthly givers. Properly handled, calls of this sort can strengthen relationships with donors by conveying to them how important their support is. Even more important, a one-off donor whose previous support has consisted of, say, three or four $25 gifts per year will become a midlevel donor if he consents to give $25 per month, or $300 per year. Even at $15 per month, that $25 donor will upgrade from $75 or $100 per year to $180. At those levels of giving, monthly donors become a major asset to a nonprofit.

You can probably think of additional ways the phone can help you get closer to your donors. Whether you yourself will have to make the calls, or either a group of volunteers or a professional agency will be doing so, it's worth considering carefully how to implement some such effort. The value of telephone contact has been proven over and over again.

But any telefundraising or telephone cultivation program brings into high relief an abiding question at most nonprofits: When all's said and done, what do we really know about our donors? If we're going to call them, what should we talk about?

This is where marketing research in its multiple forms enters the picture.

Research Without Paying Through the Nose

When the term "marketing research" comes up in conversation, I've found that most nonprofit executives tend to change the subject even more quickly than if I'd asked them for money. This phrase conjures up images of high-priced consultants charging tens of thousands of dollars to conduct surveys or focus groups, only to produce thick reports that end up on someone's shelf or in a filing cabinet stuck away in storage somewhere.

It's time to set the record straight. First, professional marketing research can answer questions about your donors, volunteers, clients, students, or any other group of constituents that you can't answer any other way. Yes, it can be significantly, even frightfully, expensive. Focus groups, surveys (whether by mail, phone, in person, or online), "mall intercepts," and other favored techniques of market researchers require lots of work by lots of people, a substantial amount of data processing, and the application of knowledge and insight that come only with years of experience—and all that costs money. But if your organization is in the big leagues (or aspires to be) and if your financial situation is secure despite external conditions, it's truly worthwhile to budget for regular marketing research.

But marketing research doesn't have to be expensive.

For starters, consider the phone calls to random donors that I mentioned in the previous section. If you standardize the questions and call enough donors within a reasonably limited period of time, you can gain a great deal of insight—if not statistically valid conclusions—about the attitudes of your donors.

However, there are more systematic ways to use the concepts of marketing research on a bare-bones budget.

Some organizations circulate surveys among their donors through inserts in newsletters. As a way to engage the small number of donors who are likely to respond, such a survey can be useful. However, it's highly risky to draw any conclusions about the organization's donors in general from such a haphazard effort. This is not the sort of thing I have in mind.

Instead, here are three possibilities you might consider:

1. **Donor or member surveys.** Marketing research agencies aren't the only possible source of professional expertise in survey research. Many academics, both at business schools and in social science departments, routinely use

high-quality survey techniques in the course of their work. At thousands of universities and other institutes of higher learning around the world, graduate students in marketing and sociology, to name just two disciplines, take courses in survey research. A scientifically designed and managed survey of your donors or members might be an attractive project for such a class. With a highly qualified instructor managing the project, your organization might receive world-class assistance in marketing research for a pittance, or even free.

2. **Donor consultation groups.** Professionally conducted focus groups cost about $6,000 in the United States, and they're not cheap anywhere else, I've found. Moreover, you can't run just one. To gain any meaningful value from focus groups, you'll need to run three or four at a minimum. But there is an alternative that my colleagues have put to work to great effect for several clients. We call it a "donor consultation group." Superficially, such a group appears similar to a focus group: it involves (ideally) ten or twelve donors or members; it lasts an hour and a half to two hours; it's typically held in the late afternoon or early evening, to permit both working donors and older folks to attend; and there is a carefully constructed questionnaire the moderator uses to guide the conversation. For a national organization, such groups need to be conducted in at least two cities. And drawing conclusions of any sort from just one or two donor con-

sultation groups would be highly risky. Be sure to conduct three or more. That's where the similarities stop, though. No professional moderator is involved. The session is held not in a specialized facility that allows onlookers to listen in on the conversation without being observed themselves but in an informal setting at a hotel or restaurant over tea and coffee or dessert. And instead of just including the moderator, a couple of the nonprofit's staff members sit in on the group. They stay silent until shortly before the end, when the moderator cues them to give a brief presentation about a particular project or program that the moderator has been discussing with the participants. (We've used this format to explore donors' receptivity to legacy giving, for example.) If the moderator is skillful—some professional background or training wouldn't hurt—a donor consultation group can yield the sort of insightful comments by donors who participate, all the while it serves as a bonding experience. Almost invariably, one or more of the participants will give an extra gift shortly after a successful donor consultation group.

3. **Online focus groups, discussion boards, or surveys.** Marketing research online can be very cheap when you do the work yourself. If you have a substantial number of online supporters, you can learn a lot about their attitudes and preferences from such activities. But it's not wise to regard the findings of online research as applying

to your donor base as a whole. Research shows that the demographic profile of online donors is significantly different from that of donors acquired through other channels.

Marketing research of this sort, whether it's formal or informal, is intended to answer questions about the attitudes, beliefs, and preferences of either your donors in general or of one or more specific segments of donors or other supporters. It can be at least equally productive to use somewhat similar techniques to learn more about your individual donors. That's the subject I take up in the following chapter.

CHAPTER 12

Get Personal with Your Donors

The problem with collecting information about your donors is that you've got to have someplace to store it, analyze it, and retrieve it. So don't even think about trying this at home unless you've got a top-notch donor file management system that's either got lots of room for detailed data entry already or the flexibility to allow you to add fields to record it.

I'll assume, though, that you've got what it takes to undertake a systematic effort to acquire personal information about your donors. This is a five-step process.

Step 1: Design a Questionnaire

The first order of business is to design a questionnaire. The information you seek might include any or all of the following items from each donor:

- Why he supports your organization—specifically (for example, if your organization conducts research into heart disease, has he or a member of his immediate family suffered from heart disease?)
- Which programs, projects, or issues you address are the most important to him
- How highly he values the benefits and services you offer
- Whether your organization is one of his top three philanthropic priorities
- Whether he actively uses e-mail (and will supply an e-mail address)
- Whether he's planning to remember your organization in his will or estate plan or is interested in learning more about that option
- How old he is (either within a date range, or, preferably, his birth date)
- His marital status, and whether there are children in the family who are living at home or living outside the home
- Optionally, within what range his household income falls

Don't confuse questions of this sort with the no-brainer options ("Is dying bad?") in those phony surveys used so widely by many nonprofit organizations. These are authentic surveys, and experience shows donors treat them as such.

Step 2: Test the Questionnaire

Once the questionnaire is drafted, step 2 is to test it. Solicit feedback from colleagues, friends, family members—anyone who can identify any ambiguous or unclear questions. Don't skimp on this step. A question you thought perfectly clear could be monumentally confusing to others.

Step 3: Prepare the Direct Mail Package

Step 3 is to include the questionnaire in a direct mail package, along with a cover letter and a preaddressed reply envelope. I came across a particularly brilliant example of such a survey in Australia, created by my friends at Pareto Fundraising for the Cancer Council New South Wales. This package contained the following items:

- A white window outer envelope
- A personalized two-page letter from Dr. Andrew Penman, chief executive officer
- A six-panel survey brochure, with each panel the same size as the letter
- A self-addressed reply envelope

For a look at the cover of the survey itself, see Figure 12.1. The text of the survey itself follows, and the final page is shown in Figure 12.2.

FIGURE 12.1 Cover of Donor Survey

"I feel really blessed to be alive. Everyday is special. I'll never take life for granted again."

Molly Stacey,
Breast Cancer Survivor

THE CANCER COUNCIL NSW
2007 SUPPORTER SURVEY

To be completed by Mr Sample by 28 February 2007.

Thank you so much for taking part in this short but vital survey.

Compassionate supporters like you have helped make The Cancer Council NSW the leading independent provider of cancer support and funding for research in Australia.

Now, by taking part in our first ever Supporters' Survey, you can help us take the next step in the ongoing battle to defeat cancer.

Your answers will help us provide more support for your community and more funds for cancer research. In short, they could help to shape the direction of our work for years to come. That's why it's so important that you take part.

IMPORTANT: Your survey will not be seen by anyone outside of The Cancer Council. So please answer as many questions as possible – the more information you provide, the more we will be able to do to defeat cancer in our children's lifetime.

Thank you for your help.

The Cancer Council
New South Wales

Building a Cancer Smart Community

989

Section 1

The Cancer Council in NSW

1. The Cancer Council NSW provides many services to the community in NSW. Which of the following are you aware of? (*Please tick all that apply.*)

- [ ] Funds and conducts cancer research
- [ ] Provides cancer information to patients and families
- [ ] Provides support for people with cancer
- [ ] Acts independently on cancer matters
- [ ] Conducts cancer prevention campaigns
- [ ] Sells sun protection products
- [ ] Speaks up for the rights and interests of the community in relation to cancer
- [ ] Other (*Please specify.*)

_____

2. Our mission at The Cancer Council NSW is to help as many people as possible avoid, cope with, and be cured of cancer. Have you or your family benefited from the activities of The Cancer Council?

- [ ] Yes
- [ ] No

3. If yes, in which of the following ways have you benefited? (*Please tick all that apply.*)

- [ ] Used their information services
- [ ] Benefited from education or prevention campaigns
- [ ] Used their support services
- [ ] Used The Cancer Council help line

☐ Benefited from advocacy campaigns like smoke free pubs or patient rights

4. Which of these statements do you feel apply to The Cancer Council? (*Please tick all that apply.*)

☐ They speak out on issues of importance.

☐ They are active in my community.

☐ They are reliant on volunteers.

☐ I know people who have been helped by them.

☐ They have made a difference to my life.

☐ They have an office in my region.

Section 2

Your Experience with Cancer

5. It's important to understand how many of our supporters have been touched by cancer so that we can promote our support and research programs effectively. Have you been directly or indirectly affected by cancer?

☐ Yes

☐ No

6. If yes, who was affected? You can select more than one.

☐ Myself

☐ Parent

☐ Partner

☐ Son or daughter

☐ Friend

☐ Grandparent

☐ Other close family

☐ Work colleague

☐ Other (*Please specify.*)

Section 3

Your Support of The Cancer Council NSW

7. Understanding more about your support of The Cancer Council NSW will help our fundraising and communications program be more effective, meaning more funds can be spent on defeating cancer. Which of the following reasons best describes why you support The Cancer Council NSW?

☐ I know someone who has been affected by cancer.

☐ I just want to do something to stop people from getting cancer.

☐ I enjoy The Cancer Council events.

☐ It is one of several charities I support.

☐ They are a trustworthy organization doing good work.

8. Which area of The Cancer Council activities do you personally feel is the most important? (*Please tick one only.*)

☐ Campaigns to prevent cancer

☐ Support and information services for cancer patients

☐ Conducting cancer research

☐ Advocating for policies and programs for cancer prevention, treatment, and support

9. Automatic small monthly donations deducted from your bank account or credit cards are the most effective ways to support The Cancer Council NSW's work. Monthly donations help us budget and plan our long-term research and support programs. Would you consider making an automatic small monthly donation to The Cancer Council NSW?

☐ Yes, I would be interested in making automatic small monthly donations—please contact me.

☐ Possibly, please provide me with more information.

☐ I already make automatic monthly donations to The Cancer Council NSW.

10. Bequests left to The Cancer Council NSW by people in their wills are of enormous benefit to our research and support programs. It is important to know how many people support us in this way. Have you written The Cancer Council NSW in your will?

☐ Yes, I have already mentioned The Cancer Council NSW in my will.

☐ I intend to include The Cancer Council NSW when I next revise my will.

☐ I would consider including The Cancer Council NSW in my will and would like more information.

☐ I do not have a will.

☐ I have written a will and have mentioned charities but do not intend to include The Cancer Council NSW in my will.

☐ I have written a will but have chosen not to mention charities.

11. Every year, The Cancer Council NSW organizes a series of fundraising events. These events are vital in supporting our research and support programs and are easy and great fun to participate in. Please indicate if you are interested in receiving more information on the following events in 2007, and we will contact you nearer the time.

☐ Australia's Biggest Morning Tea—24th May (Everyone loves a break: get your friends/family/colleagues together and have a "cuppa" for cancer!)

☐ Daffodil Day—24th August (With you we have hope: Show support for those affected by cancer and simply order fresh daffodils and merchandise.)

☐ Girls Night Out—1st October (Get the girls together for a Girls Night In, and help raise funds for women's cancer.)

☐ Pink Ribbon Day—22nd October (Breast cancer is the most common cancer for women in Australia. Order your box of Pink Ribbons to show support.)

☐ Relay for Life—coming soon to an oval near you; a fun, outdoor, and overnight fundraising event you'll never forget. A place you can join your community in the fight against cancer. A day filled with fun, festivities, and a place to make friends, a day to honor those who have survived cancer and remember those we've lost.

12. The Cancer Council NSW is reliant on volunteers to assist with education programs, campaigns, support services, and helping out in our offices throughout NSW. Would you be interested in receiving an information packet about Cancer Council volunteer opportunities?

☐ Yes

☐ No

13. The Cancer Council NSW undertakes advocacy campaigns aimed at improving services and support for cancer patients and for policies to protect people from cancer. Would you be interested in advocating for The Cancer Council NSW in the following areas?

☐ Tobacco control issues

☐ Lifestyle issues like nutrition and sun protection

☐ Improved treatment and services

☐ Local cancer issues

☐ Please send me the Cancer Action newsletter

14. We are grateful to you for all the support you have provided in the past. Are you planning to remain a supporter of The Cancer Council NSW?

☐ Yes, for the foreseeable future

☐ Yes, for at least the year ahead

☐ Don't know

☐ No

15. If you answered "No" or "Don't know" to the above question, please tell us why in the box below.

_____

_____

_____

_____

_____

16. Which other charities do you support?

☐ Heart Foundation

☐ Children's Cancer Institute Australia

☐ Christian Blind Mission International

☐ Child Fund Australia

☐ Vision Australia

☐ MS Society

☐ Alzheimer's Australia

☐ Starlight Foundation

☐ Australian Red Cross

☐ Children's Hospital Westmead

☐ Leukemia Foundation

☐ Australian Cancer Research Foundation

☐ Fred Hollows Foundation

☐ National Breast Cancer Foundation

☐ The Sydney Children's Hospital

☐ Salvation Army

☐ World Vision

☐ Other (*Please specify*)

_____

Section 4

About You

To help put your answers into context, it really helps to know a little about you. Please rest assured that the information you provide remains confidential and will be used by The Cancer Council NSW only for the purposes of improving our communications with you, and our work in general.

● ● ●

17. Do you rent or own the home you live in?

☐ I rent.

☐ I am an owner with no mortgage.

☐ I own, but still have a mortgage.

18. What is your approximate annual household income?

☐ Up to $10,000 $10,001– $20,000

☐ $20,001– $30,000 $30,001– $40,000

☐ $40,001– $60,000 $60,001– $80,000

☐ $80,001– $100,000 $100,001–$150,000

☐ $150,001– $200,000 $200,001+

19. How many children and/or grandchildren under the age of 18 do you have?

☐ _____ Children   _____ Grandchildren

20. What age are your children and grandchildren?

☐ Child 1   Grandchild 1

☐ Child 2   Grandchild 2

☐ Child 3   Grandchild 3

☐ Child 4   Grandchild 4

☐ Child 5   Grandchild 5

21. Which of the following best describes your relationship status?

☐ Single

☐ Married/de facto

☐ Divorced or separated

☐ Widowed

22. Please state your gender.

☐ Male   ☐ Female

23. Providing us with your birth date helps ensure your privacy when you contact us, as we release personal details only once your date of birth has been verified. Please provide your date of birth below.

_____ / _____ / _____ (dd/mm/yy)

24. Do you use e-mail regularly?

□ Yes

□ No

25. Please provide your e-mail address below, as this can help keep our costs down if we need to contact you.

_____

26. As mobile phones are used increasingly by our supporters, it's important we keep a record of our supporters' mobile phone numbers so we can keep in contact with you this way. Please provide your mobile phone number below.

_____

27. If you have been personally touched by cancer, would you be happy for us to use your personal story in any of our future communications to supporters and members of the public? The bravery of supporters in sharing their stories greatly assists in increasing the awareness of the issues facing people with cancer, and how The Cancer Council NSW can help and support them. If you would like to share your story please indicate below.

□ Yes, I would like to share my story with others, please contact me.

28. We always welcome feedback at the cancer Council NSW. If there is anything else you would like to share with us, please do so in the space below. Thank you.

_____

_____

_____

_____

_____

_____

• • •

Privacy Information: At The Cancer Council of NSW, we recognize the importance of your privacy and the safeguarding of your personal information. We are careful with all of your details and will use them to contact you about fundraising, our work, events, merchandise, and other issues we believe will be important to you. You can change type and frequency of information you receive from us by simply calling us on 1300 780 113. Thank you.

FIGURE 12.2 Sixth Panel of Donor Survey

This year in NSW more than 30,000 people will be diagnosed with cancer.

DO WE HAVE YOUR CORRECT CONTACT DETAILS?
Please fill in any blanks, and correct any errors in the box below. Thank you.

Mr Albert Sample
123 Sample Street
SAMPLEVILLE SAM 0000

In Honour

999 / XX0899 / X899

Do we have your correct contact details? Please fill in any blanks, and correct any errors in the box below. Thank you.

Title: First Name: Surname:

Address:

Phone: (h)   (w)

YOUR SUPPORT

**Any additional donations that you can make at this stage will also really help us defeat cancer.
Please return the survey with a gift of whatever you can afford – your ongoing support is much
appreciated by The Cancer Council NSW and the people who rely on us.**

I want to make a donation in support of The Cancer Council...

☐ $0, enough to provide 0 callers to The Cancer Council's Helpline with practical and
   emotional support to help them cope along their cancer journey

☐ $0, enough to distribute up-to-date information to cancer patients, medical practitioners and the
   general community about cancer prevention, treatment and care

☐ $0, enough to pay for some of the vital laboratory equipment that could help uncover new cancer
   treatments and cures

☐ My choice $_____

I prefer to give by: ☐ Visa   ☐ MasterCard   ☐ Amex   ☐ Diners
                       ☐ Cheque/Money Order *(made payable to The Cancer Council NSW)*

Credit Card Number: ☐☐☐☐ ☐☐☐☐ ☐☐☐☐ ☐☐☐☐   Expiry date: ☐☐ ☐☐

Card holder's name: _____

Signature: _____

**Thank you. Please return this survey in the enclosed envelope to:
2007 Supporter Survey, Andrew Penman, Chief Executive Officer,
Reply Paid 572 KINGS CROSS NSW 1340**

Privacy Information: At The Cancer Council of NSW we recognise the importance of your privacy and the safeguarding of your personal information.
We are careful with all of your details and will use them to contact you about fundraising, our work, events, merchandise and other issues we believe will
be important to you. You can change the type and frequency of information you receive from us by simply calling us on 1300 780 113. Thank you.
ABN. 51 116 463 946

6MAIN

Step 4: Mail the Questionnaire Package to Your Donors

Ideally, in step 4, you'll mail this package to all of your donors. If a mailing of that size is beyond your means, then choose the top donor segments of your database.

Step 5: Enter the Information on Your Donor Database

If all goes well, you'll receive a substantial response. In previous years, I've witnessed response rates of between 20 and 30 percent. However, it might be prudent to scale back your expectations during challenging times. Ten percent might be a safer level to plan for. In any case, you'll need to be prepared in advance for step 5, which is to enter all the data on individual records in your database—and without delay.

Now comes the key to the whole exercise: step 6, which is to *make use of the information.*

Step 6: Put the Information to Work

It doesn't take a lot of imagination to understand that if you're working for a cancer research charity and you know that a donor's connection to your cause was the death of a loved one, you can write far more powerful copy. If you're promoting after-school programs for young children and a donor is either a parent or an elementary school teacher, that connection can allow you to address her in a far more personal way. And if you know that a donor regards your organization as one of his top three charities, you might assume there is a strong likelihood that he'll give serious thought to an upgrade request.

These are things we know instinctively. But except for major-donor fundraisers (who are trained to approach donors in an informed manner), we typically do a poor job of working personal information into our appeals. All too often, our mantra is, "Keep costs low." We struggle mightily to cut a penny here and a penny there from the production and mailing costs of our direct mail packages. We haggle endlessly with telefundraising agencies to lower the cost per contact. We frequently shun even the most rudimentary personalization (name, address, and giving level) because that will add to the costs of our direct mail or phone appeals. (There's no direct cost to personalize e-mails, only technical issues that may entail indirect costs.) Yet by making cost rather than cost-effectiveness the guiding principle in our communications with donors, we lose the use of the fundraiser's most powerful tool: *the ability to appeal directly to an individual donor's cherished values and beliefs.*

Consider how we might make use of the information acquired by the Cancer Council New South Wales in subsequent communications with donors. Let's assume that 30,000 individuals received the survey appeal presented in this chapter and that 10,000 of them responded. Let's also assume that 8,000 of those sent gifts with their surveys. We'll stipulate further that all of the 10,000 respondents answered question 5, with 5,000 of them saying they had been directly or indirectly affected by cancer and the other 5,000 indicating they hadn't. For an overview of this information, take a look at Table 12.1.

As you can see, an appeal to the same 30,000 Cancer Council donors might be split into five segments, with donors affected by cancer in one segment, those unaffected in a second, nondonors who are affected in a third, nondonors who are not affected in a fourth, and nonrespondents in a fifth segment.

- The lead for segment 1 might begin as follows: "Thank you so very much for responding to my survey last month and for your generous gift of $[AMT]. Because you have shared with me the sad fact that your life has been affected by cancer, I know that . . ."
- For segment 2, the lead would begin: "Thank you so very much for responding to our survey last month and for your generous gift of $[AMT]."

TABLE 12.1 Segmentation of Cancer Council Donors Following a Survey Mailing

Segment Number	Respondent?	Donor?	Affected?
1		Yes—8,000	Yes—4,000
2	Yes—10,000		No—4,000
3		No—2,000	Yes—1,000
4			No—1,000
5	No—20,000	No	?

- Respondents in segment 3 would receive a letter beginning: "Thank you so very much for responding to my survey last month. Because you have shared with me the sad fact that your life has been affected by cancer, I know that . . ."
- The lead for Segment 4 might start with the following words: "Thank you so very much for responding to my survey last month."
- Segment 5 would receive an appeal with a lead that contains no such personalization.

In reality, this segmentation would be overlaid on a more general segmentation along the lines of the recency-frequency-giving level model I discussed earlier. The result would be a far more complex segmentation plan. And that approach deals only with one of the questions in the survey! The more such sensitive, truly personal information you can work into a direct marketing appeal, the higher the response is likely to go. Fundraising letters constructed along these lines have been known to double or triple the income from similar but nonpersonalized appeals.

Is this sort of thing easy to do? No, of course not. It requires considerable patience and persistence—and a lot of work to craft appeals that might have dozens or even more than a hundred distinct copy segments. But is it worth the effort? Can it possibly justify what might be significant investment in printing and mailing costs, data entry, and possibly other new costs?

Yes. A thousand times yes, assuming you're not so strapped for cash that you're having trouble meeting payroll. Try it, and you'll see your fundraising revenue soar.

And while you're at it, consider how a little extra effort online might boost your revenue even further. We delve into that subject in the following chapter.

CHAPTER 13

Step Up Your Efforts Online

L et's get something straight right off the bat. If what you've got in mind is to cut costs in direct mail and other forms of capital-intensive fundraising and substitute online communications instead, forget it. This course will lead to grief. I know of at least one organization, consumed by a rigid environmental ethic, that eliminated its direct mail program entirely a few years ago and switched to fundraising by e-mail. It shut its doors within a year.

Online fundraising and communications is an exciting field brimming over with promise. You can recruit new supporters, including donors; you can engage and motivate your donors; you can even raise a little money. But you can't expect donors to change their habits overnight and respond online to the same sort of appeals that you might otherwise deliver by phone or mail. And don't hold your breath waiting for millions to pour in from your Facebook Cause or in response to Twitter tweets. Those things simply ain't going to happen. By 2020, perhaps, but not in the foreseeable future, despite all the rosy predictions from the online-fundraising boosters club. And certainly not soon enough to help you compensate for shortfalls in other aspects of your fundraising program caused by prevailing economic conditions.

But here's what you *can* expect from the online medium today:

- Studies show that a hugely disproportionate number of donors—*your* donors!—use e-mail and the Internet— 80 percent of them in one notable study. They may not be giving to you now, but they're likely to be more receptive to communicating with you online than you think they are.
- Research indicates that half of all those who receive appeals for funds from nonprofit organizations go first to the Internet to check their Web sites. Some, a much smaller proportion, also check the sites of the charity watchdogs such as GuideStar, Charity Navigator, and the Better Business Bureau Wise Giving Alliance. More and more, donors are even giving online in response to appeals sent through direct mail. My colleagues and I have been seeing as much as 10 to 20 percent of revenue from direct mail renewals or special appeals come in online for organizations that have strong Web sites.

- The experience of fundraisers who are using e-mail to reinforce direct mail or telefundraising efforts clearly suggests that e-mail boosts overall response without necessarily bringing in much money online.
- Increasingly, special events are taking shape online. Invitations, registration, and payment can all be handled with great efficiency over the Internet, and as a result some organizations now use the online medium exclusively to promote and organize their events.

Just to be clear now: while I've been the principal of a direct mail fundraising agency for thirty years at this writing, I've been professionally engaged in online fundraising for about half as long (and in telephone fundraising much longer than that). I strongly believe that over the long run, fundraisers will come to rely on online communications to bring in a disproportionate share of revenue—while playing an ever more prominent role in reinforcing fundraising efforts through other channels in the short run.

There are three strategic drivers of success in online fundraising:

1. A compelling and involving Web site that cries out to visitors to become engaged—to give if possible, but at the very least to leave their e-mail addresses.
2. An ongoing effort to acquire e-mail addresses through every means possible. Only with a large and growing e-mail list can your organization thrive online.

3. An easy way for visitors—and especially donors acquired through other channels—to contribute through your Web site. Increasingly, direct mail–acquired donors are developing the habit of renewing or making special contributions online in response to direct mail appeals.

   With that understanding, let's begin by reviewing fifteen of the simple steps you can take online—without spending much, if any, money—to support your fundraising program:

1. If you don't already produce an electronic or e-newsletter or frequent alert, start one. Be sure to use your Web site to promote this opportunity to all visitors, casual or not—and invite them to sign up free of charge and with minimal fuss and bother. (The less information you ask for, the more people will sign up.)
2. Use every opportunity to gather e-mail addresses from your supporters, and immediately add each new address to your e-newsletter or other e-mail communication. This means including a line for donors and prospects to write in an e-mail address on every form you distribute, whether through the mail, at your office or other facilities, or at special events. It also means sending an automatic message of thanks to every new subscriber, with one or more links to pages on your Web site where you offer news or opportunities for engagement.

3. If you're contacting your supporters once a month by e-mail, increase the frequency to twice monthly or weekly. If you've secured permission from your supporters to contact them by e-mail, you'll probably find that only a small percentage will "unsubscribe."

4. Optimize online giving opportunities on your Web site by making the process as easy as possible for donors. For example, include a prominent Donate button on every page—including, of course, your home page.

5. Include a Donate button on every e-mail you send—including those from staff (and that means you too!). Be sure you don't overlook your e-newsletter.

6. Develop a "get-a-friend" capacity, offering readers the option to forward your content to friends, and include it in every e-mail communication—newsletter, alert, whatever. If your online communications are powerful, and especially if your work or the issue you address is prominent in the news, you might acquire a substantial number of new supporters through such referrals.

7. Build a specific landing page for each electronic appeal to reinforce the specific case for giving. Don't merely send prospective donors to your standard donation page. This would be the equivalent in direct mail of enclosing a standard wallet-flap remittance envelope with every fundraising letter—which (I hope I needn't add) is a big no-no.

8. If your organization is engaged even slightly in policy advocacy, design a petition to gather e-mail addresses, thus building your list. If advocacy is foreign to your organization, try a contest or a quiz about the issues you address. An intriguing petition, contest, or quiz might attract hundreds or thousands of new supporters as it bounces around the ozone.

9. Make sure you're using the capability of your online fundraising tools to track donor interests and behaviors, and be sure to use that information to personalize your e-mail offers. For example, consider sending an online survey (using a service such as SurveyMonkey or Zoomerang) to elicit some of the same sort of information I noted in Chapter Twelve, and integrate the answers into e-mail communications.

10. Precede every appeal by mail or phone with an e-mail message to all donors selected for inclusion in the project. You could send either a simple heads-up notice that an urgent letter is in the mail—or you could give those who prefer to contribute online a chance to save you the expense of mailing them by giving online. Either way, you're likely to boost the returns you receive in the mail. You might also consider following up an appeal by mail or phone with a second e-mail, updating donors on the progress of your fundraising campaign and giving them one more chance to contribute to it.

11. Convert online donors to monthly sustainers. Almost everywhere outside the United States, nearly all fundraisers know that one-off gifts are a far less reliable and less lucrative source of support for nonprofit initiatives than are regular or committed monthly donors. Equally important, monthly donors are on average far more loyal than one-off donors. It's not unusual for monthly givers to continue contributing—and, in many cases, regularly increasing—their gifts for ten years or longer. Despite resistance from many American banks, hundreds of venturesome nonprofits have succeeded in converting a large enough proportion of their donors (perhaps 10 to 20 percent) to monthly programs, so that their gifts account for as much as half the overall income from membership or direct marketing. In Europe, by contrast, many nonprofits exist almost exclusively on the basis of committed giving. Although relatively few online donors are likely to convert to a monthly program, the cost of offering them the opportunity is low. And those who do buy in become the backbone of an online fundraising program.

12. Apply for a Google Grant. You're eligible if your organization is a U.S. 501(c)(3) and shares Google's "philosophy of community service to help the world in areas such as science and technology, education, global public health, the environment, youth advocacy, and the

arts." If you are approved, a Google Grant will provide you with free search AdWords. When a keyword related to your organization or your issue is searched, a small text ad like the following will appear in the upper-right-hand column. Here is what appears when I searched for "torture":

Sponsored Links

1. <u>Waterboarding Is Torture</u>

Join Us Today to Stop the Cruel
Practice of **Torture**!
www.HumanRightsFirst.org

13. Develop a "charity badge" or "widget"—a small, colorful link to your Web site—that your supporters can place on their Facebook, MySpace, or other social networking pages. If your widget is clever and attention getting and enough of your supporters agree to post it, you can significantly boost traffic to your site. Figure 13.1 shows the charity badge I picked up from the Facebook page of the Humane Society of the United States.

14. Take a page from the playbook of the word-of-mouth marketers, and ask your supporters to write brief statements of support for your organization and its work. Post the best of them online. If you get enough, create a separate page linked to the home page, offering "What They Say About Us." Testimonials by clients or benefi-

FIGURE 13.1 Humane Society Charity Badge

ciaries, donors, volunteers, or community members can
be far more effective in making your case for giving
than you can manage. They're simply more credible.

15. To take the word-of-mouth concept a step further, sign
up your organization with Great Nonprofits
(www.greatnonprofits.org). There, your donors, volunteers, and other stakeholders can register their comments about the experiences they've had with your
organization. You'll get more exposure, which will lead
to more traffic on your Web site—and potentially more
donors. (Don't worry about negative comments. There

may well be a few, but they're inevitably far outnumbered by the positive ones. In today's skeptical society, you probably will even need a few nasty remarks to make the nice ones credible!)

Those are among the cheap options—especially attractive in a down economy. If, despite economic conditions, you have the necessary financial resources to bolster your online program, there are many other steps you can consider taking. Here are six possibilities:

1. If you are rejected for a Google Grant, you should consider buying AdWords on Google and possibly other widely used search engines. This practice has proven to be one of the most productive ways to advertise online— usually far more so than the familiar, but now old-fashioned, banner ads.
2. The process of search engine optimization (SEO) normally requires either a savvy in-house Webmaster or professional help—or both. It takes time. (SEO involves tweaking code throughout your site that will greatly increase the chances that search engines will list your site in a higher position when people search for "your" keywords.) The payoff comes in an increased flow of visits to your Web site by people who access one or another of the major search engines.

3. Increase the frequency of changes you make to your Web site, especially the home page. If you post new articles, videos, testimonials, or other new items on a weekly basis instead of monthly, or daily instead of weekly, your search engine ranking—and thus, in all likelihood, the traffic to your site—will increase. This, of course, means extra work for someone, and possibly even an extra staff position.

4. Produce videos that deliver up-to-the-minute information about your work. These can be as simple as talking-head updates or as elaborate as a Hollywood production. Posted on a Web site or distributed by e-mail, a video is likely to gain you far more attention than even an article. More people now watch video online than use search engines.

5. Take a hint from MoveOn.org and the Obama campaign and set modest, short-term fundraising goals that will lend themselves to day-long or week-long campaigns. Engineer a real-time progress report to keep up the momentum as new donors join in the effort.

6. Try paid "chaperoned e-mails"—appeals from your organization that are sent by intermediary organizations (such as media sites) to their subscribers. If the cause or issue you're addressing is consistent with the values and demographic profile of the subscribers to that site or service, you might attract a significant number of new names

for your list. But don't expect to ask them for money, at least not initially. This is a list-building exercise. You'll have to work on inducing them to become donors.

Actions along these lines will yield two significant dividends for your organization. First, your relationships with your donors will be strengthened, because you'll be broadening a channel of communications they can exploit to become more engaged in advancing your mission. And second, you'll be laying the groundwork for your future fundraising, which will almost certainly rest more squarely on electronic communications than on traditional mail and phone. But there is an even more significant step involving e-mail and the Internet that you can take to boost your fundraising program: break down the silos within your development operations and between development, communications, and marketing. We'll take up that subject in the next chapter.

CHAPTER 14

Break Down the Silos

The world is closing in around you. Business as usual simply won't cut it in the midst of the most challenging economic conditions in nearly a century. Your organization has got to find ways to work better, faster, and cheaper.

Before you embark on any further steps, take this pop quiz:

• • •

Which, if any, of the following statements are true about your organization? Check all those that apply:

• • •

☐ You have a talented marketing department that does great work, but the head of marketing doesn't get along with the head of fundraising. In fact, they can barely stand to be in a room together.

☐ The person in charge of major gifts looks down her nose at direct mail (and won't even allow telemarketing to be mentioned in her presence). The degree of cooperation between the major gifts officers and the direct marketing people is either run quietly through a backchannel or is nil.

☐ Your Web site—in fact, almost all online communications— is managed by either an office dedicated to online operations or a communications department, and it's like pulling teeth for people in other departments to get them to consider anything but their own ideas.

☐ Your performance, and that of your colleagues in your department (whichever department it is), will be evaluated exclusively in relation to your success in achieving departmental goals. The organization's overall goals are either unknown or entirely ignored except by the board.

☐ The people in the legacy or planned giving office are all high-priced professionals trained in accounting, the law, or financial services, and they couldn't care less what a bottom-feeder such as a direct mail fundraiser might have to say about marketing legacy gifts.

☐ The folks engaged in institutional fundraising (foundations and corporations) have never considered the possibility that some of the donors—even small donors—to

your organization might have valuable connections
with institutional funders through family, friends,
neighbors, or coworkers.

☐ Life used to be simple back when there was only one
database—or at most two. Now every department has its
own: membership or direct marketing, major gifts,
legacy giving, online communications.

If you checked off even one of those admitted over-
drawn statements, I suspect you realize that your organization
has a problem. Potentially, a very big problem.

Commercial marketers have known for many years
that buyers don't fit themselves neatly into silos. They understand that people are extraordinarily diverse. That some rich
folks are skinflints while poor people may be spendthrifts. That
people's circumstances change over time. That yesterday's
super-shopper may become tomorrow's shut-in. That no company "owns" a customer, who may shop from a dozen, or a
dozen times a dozen, other shops, catalogues, and Web sites.
That even the members of a single family may have markedly
different media habits, with some members preferring information that arrives by TV, others the newspaper or magazines,
and yet others the mail or the phone or online. And that getting
a message through the extraordinary clutter in our airwaves, our
mailboxes, and our ever-more-addled brains requires that we
repeat and repeat and repeat again—and use every available
communications channel to the fullest possible extent.

Despite these lessons, all of them obvious in hindsight, far too many nonprofit organizations are structured in such a way as to make implementing those insights virtually impossible.

Here's the down-and-dirty reality about your donors—and just about everyone else's:

- Precious few donors begin their philanthropic behavior with big gifts. Almost invariably they start small, perhaps even with gifts of $15 or $20. Some are testing the organization, waiting to see how it responds to a small contribution. Others simply are cautious about committing themselves before they've gotten a meaningful sense of how the organization operates. Still others start out poor and later make more money. In fact, in the United States, the largest single proportion of first-time donors responded to a direct mail solicitation—probably with gifts of less than $100. And the corollary to this proposition is that the overwhelming majority of major donors originally come from the ranks of direct mail or other direct marketing contributors.
- The best estimates I can find make it clear that at least 80 percent, and probably 90 percent or more, of legacy gifts are simple bequests. And those bequests—which average $35,000 in the United States, $30,000 in Canada, $20,000 in Australia, and $18,000 in the United Kingdom—are significant contributions in anybody's

book. For most nonprofit organizations in the United States, despite the often much larger size of the charitable trusts and other complex instruments that preoccupy planned giving officers, the majority of legacy income is derived from bequests. And—you guessed it—those bequests *do not* tend to come from major donors. They come from the same small-donor pool as most major cash donors—individuals who most often are recruited through direct marketing. Studies show that there is virtually no correlation whatsoever between the size of a person's assets and the propensity to leave a legacy gift. In other words, poor and middle-class people are at least as intent on leaving legacies as the wealthier folks typically chased by planned giving officers.

- Donors in the midrange of giving levels are probably falling through the cracks. If your organization runs a direct marketing program on any significant scale, chances are strong you have a barbell-shaped distribution of donors: a cluster of major donors at the high end who account for a disproportionate share of your net revenue, with a comparatively huge number of small donors at the low end, and an underdeveloped middle between the two—from, say, $100 to $1,000, or from $1,000 to $25,000, depending on the character and size of your development program. This is not a natural state of affairs. In nearly every case I've observed firsthand, it's the result of a disconnect between the direct marketing

or membership department and the major gifts staff.
In nearly all cases, there's a threshold amount (often
$1,000) at or beyond which donors are off-limits to the
direct marketers. And the work of major gift officers
being what it is—time intensive—those donors who cross
the threshold may be largely, even completely, ignored,
since the major giving department is forced to concen-
trate its efforts on donors of $5,000, $10,000, or more.

- Fundraisers normally regard donors as "direct mail
donors," "telephone donors," or "online donors." It's certainly true that a large proportion of donors tend to fall
into the habit of responding largely or exclusively
through one channel, but that doesn't mean that they
receive communications through only that channel. In
fact—surprise!—most people in North America and
Europe, and among educated folks all over the world,
tend to communicate by mail, telephone, online, and
face-to-face. They read newspapers or magazines or
online newsletters. They listen to radio. They watch
TV or online video. And the more of these channels a
fundraiser can exploit with a well-conceived and well-
coordinated message, the more money he's likely to raise.

These are just a few of the reasons that compartmen-
talized or "silo-ized" fundraising makes no sense whatsoever.
Your donors are a dynamic and multidimensional con-
stituency. Regard them holistically, treat them as being sta-

tioned temporarily at one point or another along a continuum of giving, and address them as individuals in as personalized a manner as possible. That's the only way to build truly strong relationships with your donors and maximize your income in the long run.

To begin the long process of breaking down the silos, here are four substantive actions you can put in motion with (one hopes) the least disruption and fuss:

- Integrate your direct response fundraising efforts. Combine direct mail, online, and telephone fundraising efforts in carefully sequenced campaigns that will allow each effort to reinforce the others. For example, at year end, when you're likely to make the biggest push for contributions from your donors, design an integrated direct response campaign instead of isolated efforts by mail, phone, and online. Settle on an overall monetary goal, give the campaign a name, and determine a deadline. Launch the campaign with an e-mail message, followed a few days later by a first direct mail letter, then after ten days or so a round of telephone contacts and a second e-mail, with a second letter a couple of weeks after that. Conclude the series with a third and final e-mail message. The sequence might look something like the pattern described in Table 14.1.
- Work out an agreement between your direct marketing or membership staff and the major gift and legacy depart-

TABLE 14.1 A Hypothetical Integrated Direct Response Fundraising Campaign at Year-End

When	What	To Whom	Notes
Early November	E-mail announcement	All donors with e-mail addresses	Announce name, goal, deadline, benefits
Mid-November	First mailing	High-value donors	Highly personalized*
		Other active donors	Generic appeal
		Lapsed donors	Generic reactivation effort
Late November	Telefundraising	High-value and selected active donors	Report progress of campaign; announce challenge grant if possible
Around December 1	E-mail follow-up	All donors with e-mail addresses	Report progress of campaign; promote challenge grant
Early December	Second mailing	High-value nonresponding donors	Highly personalized*
		Selected active nonresponders	Personalized
Mid-December	E-mail follow-up	All nonresponders with e-mail addresses	Report progress is near goal and deadline
December 30	E-mail follow-up	All nonresponders with e-mail addresses	Last chance!

*"Highly personalized" denotes messages that include many different elements from the donor database, as compared to those that are simply "personalized" and may contain nothing more than a donor's name and one or two other personal references.

ments to avoid letting any donors fall through the cracks. Determine whether midrange donors are in fact getting short shrift because major gift officers are unable to devote the necessary time to contact them. If so, jointly design a high-dollar direct response program, using mail, phone, and online contact, to ensure that midlevel donors stay in close touch with your organization and are afforded opportunities to continue contributing.

- Integrate the separate databases your organization maintains for online and offline donors (and perhaps for major gifts, legacy giving, or other purposes as well). Integrated fundraising without an integrated database is impossible.
- Work with the executive director or CEO to set overall fundraising goals, not department-by-department objectives. If possible, develop an incentive program for everyone engaged in fundraising, marketing, and communications to attain those goals. A change like this must come from the top, of course.

My colleague Peter Schoewe related to me an interesting anecdote relating to this question. At his previous job with a large nonprofit organization, Peter said, "We had long conversations about how we could broker contact points with the donors between our different departments, that is, who would get to e-mail, phone, or mail the donors, and when. We did some benchmarking with a for-profit company, and they couldn't understand what we were getting at when we asked them how they solved that problem. Finally, they understood us, and they said, 'Oh, that's easy. Whatever is most profitable gets priority.'" As Peter emphasizes, and I wholeheartedly agree, nonprofits should base their decisions on long-term revenue goals grounded in real results rather than turf wars or worries about mistreating donors.

Will any of this come easily? Of course not! But whoever said life was easy?

Remember: no pain, no gain.

Now we're approaching the end of this litany of recommendations. In the final chapter, I'll sum them up and send you off to brave the cold, cruel world.

CHAPTER 15

Summary
Nine Practical Steps
Toward Peace of Mind

———

Several weeks and over two hundred pages ago, I set out to develop a set of recommendations for *Fundraising When Money Is Tight*. I knew then that many of my clients and other friends were losing sleep over the uncertainty about the impact of the 2008 economic meltdown on their fundraising programs, and I wanted to offer whatever advice I could to set their minds at ease. Now that you have (presumably) read through the preceding fourteen chapters, you certainly understand that I don't pretend there's any silver bullet to solve the problem. I'm not even suggesting a simple, straightforward course of action, even though you might sum it up superficially as a "selective approach," as I have done. Although some of the steps I've recommended apply specifically to fundraising during an economic downturn, you understand by now that the thrust of my argument is, for the most part, "do good fundraising." After all, when you get right down to it, when is money *not* tight in the philanthropic sector?

Just to jog your memory and reinforce that message, here are the nine practical steps I've discussed in the pages of this book.

Step 1: Reassess the whole ball of wax: fundraising, marketing, communications.

Accountability mechanisms and systematic and periodic evaluation are essential management practices—unfortunately, not universally employed in the nonprofit sector. Economic distress lays much greater urgency on the need for thorough assessment of all that we're doing. Now's the time to take advantage of the opportunity to put in place a regular process that will allow your fundraising, marketing, and communications programs to function at the highest degree of efficiency and effectiveness.

Step 2: Strengthen your case for giving.

Among the trustees of many nonprofit organizations—and, sadly, among a great many staff members as well—there is a working assumption that the public owes them a living. Too many of us in the social sector act as though the noble motives that lead us to accept lower pay and longer hours in nonprofit organizations create an obligation on the part of the public to support our efforts. This would be a laughable delusion if the belief didn't appear to be so widespread. Obviously (at least to those who have surveyed the intense competition in the nonprofit sector), we fundraisers have to be both skilled and artful in making the case for giving to our organizations. Money just doesn't materialize. It has to be earned. This lesson is dramatized by the pressures of a recession. Take advantage of it to reexamine your case for giving from top to bottom. And be certain your donors understand both the more urgent need for your services during tough times and the many concrete steps you're taking to increase your efficiency and effectiveness.

Step 3: Be content with one in the hand—forget the two that may be in the bush.

Many fundraising consultants are enamored with creativity. The people who manage nonprofit organizations are often similarly obsessed. When the creative process is used to devise a powerful marketing concept or a persuasive set of donor benefits, it's all to the good. But when flashy graphics and splashes of brightly colored ink are passed off as "creativity," there are bound to be losers all around. If the decades-long experience of direct marketers has anything at all to teach the fundraising profession, it's that different isn't always better— and that it can take years to produce better results than an old standard appeal that's been working reasonably well for a long time. An economic downturn does not justify throwing out what has worked in the past. In fact, it's a time for caution and cost cutting.

Step 4: Cut costs with a scalpel, not an ax.

There are lots of easy ways to cut costs in fundraising. You can stop prospecting for new donors. You can eliminate thank-yous to donors. You can cut out telemarketing efforts, slash the direct mail budget, and reduce the major gift staff. The only problem with this heedless approach is that it's a prescription for bankruptcy.

Business goes on whatever the economic conditions. You can't *not* raise funds. You can't treat loyal and responsive donors like statistics. And you can't stop building your donor database. If you do these things, your donor list will shrink through attrition, both natural and unnatural, and your income will slack off to a dribble.

The only defensible, businesslike way to respond to an economic crisis is to recognize that fundraising requires both continuing investment and ongoing care. If the choice arises between cutting back slightly on programs or slashing the fundraising budget, you may shoot yourself in the foot if you opt for the latter. It doesn't take much to destroy an effective fundraising operation—and *then* where will your program be?

Step 5: Fish where the big fish are.

It's obvious to anyone professionally involved in fundraising that it's generally more cost-effective to raise money in big chunks than in little ones. A grant from an institutional funder or a significant gift from an individual major donor rarely comes at a high cost of fundraising. And anyone who's attended even one fundraising conference or workshop has surely become acquainted with the Pareto principle, or 80–20 rule, which teaches us that a relatively small number of more generous donors account for the lion's share of the net philanthropic revenue our organizations receive. All of this points to the wisdom of focusing more time, effort, and money on generous and responsive donors and less on less productive ones. Yet how many nonprofit organizations truly make use of the simple donor file segmentation tools that make it possible for us to take advantage of these self-evident truths? If your organization has the habit of treating all your donors the same way, it's time to examine how you can fine-tune your program with a well-considered segmentation plan. A year or two ago, without external economic pressures, you might have been able to coast by without it. Now, in tough times, you can't afford not to adopt this fundamental fundraising practice. If you're already well acquainted with segmentation, it's time to consider focusing more on midlevel as well as major donors while raising the minimum standards for including donors in your appeals.

Step 6: Stay close to your donors.

A study of high-net-worth American donors conducted late in 2008 by the Center on Philanthropy at Indiana University for

the Bank of America revealed that the number one reason
(57.7 percent) that donors stopped giving to a particular charity was "no longer feeling connected to the organization." Is
this any surprise? (If it is, it's time for you to delve a little
deeper into the subject of donor motivation.) Donors need to
feel appreciated. They need to feel informed. Their confidence in the charity needs to be constantly reinforced. And
that's true of donors in general, not just the millionaires stud-
ied in the Bank of America project. At no time can a nonprofit organization operate as though its donors will continue
giving no matter how they're treated. During an economic
downturn, it's doubly urgent to hold your donors close to your
chest, because it's all too easy for a donor to lose a sense of
connection with you.

Step 7: Get personal with your donors.

No major gift officer worth her salt would dream of visiting a
prospect without at least attempting to uncover every possible
bit of intelligence on the prospect's giving history and personal interests (among many other things). Why, then, should
it seem unnatural for a fundraiser who deals with hundreds
or thousands of donors at a time—through the mail, phone,
or online—to gather personal information about them before
approaching them for gifts? Sadly, most direct response
fundraisers act as though this is an unnatural act. We work
from bare-bones databases. Generic appeals predominate. We
write to our "Dear Friend" or our "Dear Donor" without any

inkling of what might interest or motivate that individual. Surely we all understand that such an impersonal approach might be necessary in new-donor acquisition efforts. But don't we know more about our donors than simply that they've given us money once upon a time? If we have anything more than the most rudimentary of databases, we know how much they've given, how often, and how frequently. We know how long they've been giving to us. And we know what sort of appeal triggered their first gifts, whether it was a letter, a phone call, an e-mail, a visit to our Web site, or a conversation with a friend or acquaintance. Even if that's all the information we integrate into our appeals, surely that's got to do a better job of securing additional support than a crude "Dear Donor" letter! And since it's so simple to gather even more personal information from at least some of our donors, what's stopping us? Are we afraid of actually raising more money?

Step 8: Step up your efforts online.

For nearly two decades, since the World Wide Web went public in autumn 1992, fundraisers have been anticipating the death of direct mail and the ascendancy of fundraising online. That it hasn't yet happened seems to have surprised a lot of people (especially, it appears, members of nonprofit boards of directors). Certainly, billions of dollars have been raised online—but the lion's share of that money has gone into the coffers of humanitarian relief organizations such as the Red Cross, the Salvation Army, and UNICEF; the highest-profile

U.S. presidential campaigns, most notably Barack Obama's; and, to a lesser extent, the leading advocacy (or campaigning) organizations, such as the Human Rights Campaign, Amnesty International, and Greenpeace. And all those billions, despite how large the numbers might seem, represent a tiny fraction of philanthropic revenue generally (somewhere between 1 and 3 percent in the United States, depending on whom you ask). So online fundraising for its own sake does not represent the salvation of the nonprofit sector in a difficult economy, at least not in the short term. However, the online channel has multiple benefits for nonprofit fundraisers, and most of them have nothing to do directly with money: attracting younger supporters, providing constituents with opportunities for participation in your work, and reinforcing appeals sent through other channels, to name just three. More investment in online communications will pay many dividends, reinforcing near-term fundraising efforts in the short term and laying the foundation for a more prosperous future.

Step 9: Break down the silos.

If a whole bunch of different folks are beating up on someone, there are going to be problems. First, that someone will get beaten down by the process. That's bad enough. But some of the other folks will get tired of picking on that one poor soul and start attacking the others. If you think that description overstates the reality that exists in the fundraising, marketing, and communications efforts at, say, many major universities and other large nonprofit organizations, think again.

The communications department sends an alumna a magazine. The liberal arts college sends its solicitations a couple of times a year. The university annual fund enlists students to call her. The history department (her major) is all over her for a gift too. So is the graduate school of social science, because she received an M.A. in economics as well as her B.A. Then, of course, there's the alumni association, which is constantly mailing brochures about trips to all manner of exotic places around the world—as well as e-mails and letters about the football and basketball teams. And we mustn't forget the class reunion, which occasions appeals of its own—by e-mail, mail, and telephone.

Is it any wonder that so many universities are crying about the low rate of annual fund "participation" by their alumni?

Does this seem like any way to run a railroad?

This reality, which pertains to some degree at hundreds, if not thousands, of nonprofit organizations and institutions, cries out for a referee to minimize the midair collisions of all those messages. Some minimal degree of centralized scheduling among all these competing offices would surely reduce donor attrition. That alone would be an accomplishment. But take the logic one step further, and you'll realize that a truly integrated program of fundraising, marketing, and communications would boost revenue, even under the worst external conditions.

• • •

So if you follow every one of these nine recommendations to the letter, will the recession go away? Will you achieve fundraising nirvana?

Hardly. I offer these suggestions in hopes that you'll take my advice to heart and apply it judiciously in the context of your own organization's fundraising reality. I believe that if you do, you'll be much better positioned to maximize your income in the short run and preserve your capacity for renewed growth once economic conditions improve. In any case, I hope you'll find this message reassuring.

Sleep well. This too shall pass.

READING LIST

AFP E-Wire. "Fundraising Tips: Do's and Don'ts in a Troubled Economy." Arlington, Va.: Association of Fundraising Professionals, Sept. 22, 2008.

Allen, Nick. "Year-End Fundraising in a Down Economy." Presentation to the Nonprofit Technology Network, Oct. 31, 2008.

Andresen, Katya. "Six Ways to Survive the Economic Storm." *Katya's Non-Profit Marketing Blog,* Oct. 17, 2008.

"As Global Stock Markets Plunge, What Are the Implications for Fundraising?" Vancouver: Harvey McKinnon Associates, Oct. 2008.

"Ask the Experts." AFP *Golden Gate eBulletin,* Nov. 2008.

Belford, Tom. "Americans Surprisingly Confident." *Agitator,* Oct. 16, 2008.

Belford, Tom. "Fundraising in Tough Times for Acme Food Bank." *Agitator,* Oct. 21, 2008.

Belford, Tom. "Simply Inexcusable." *Agitator,* Dec. 2, 2008.

Belford, Tom. "Debate on Recession Fundraising Tactics." *Agitator,* Dec. 16, 2008.

Belford, Tom. "Recession Fundraising—What Your Colleagues Are Doing." *Agitator,* Dec. 19, 2008.

Belford, Tom, and Craver, Roger. "Fundraising in Tough Times." *Agitator,* Nov. 21, 2008.

Bhagat, Vinay. "Looking Back, Looking Ahead: What the Numbers Tell Us." *Convio Connection,* Jan.-Feb. 2008.

Blankinship, Donna Gordon. "Americans Still Giving, Despite Economic Meltdown." Associated Press, Nov. 21, 2008.

Blum, Debra E. "Fund-Raising Angst Backed Up by 2008 Declines in Gifts, Survey Finds." *Chronicle of Philanthropy,* Oct. 30, 2008.

Brooks, Jeff. "The Sky Is Falling: Who Cares?" Donor Power Blog, Oct. 8, 2008.

Brown, Melissa S., and Rooney, Patrick M. "Giving Following a Crisis: An Historical Analysis." Bloomington, Ind.: Center on Philanthropy at Indiana University.

Campbell-Rinker. "Donor Confidence Report." Issue 1, Rockville, Md.: Campbell-Rinker, Oct. 2008.

Canning, Doyle, and Rensborough, Patrick. "Re-Imagining Change: An Introduction to Story-Based Strategy." Smart-Meme, Nov. 2008.

Center on Philanthropy at Indiana University. "Briefing on the Economy and Charitable Giving." Bloomington, Ind.: Center on Philanthropy at Indiana University, Nov. 2008.

Center on Philanthropy at Indiana University. *Giving USA 2008: The Annual Report on Philanthropy for the Year 2008.* Bloomington, Ind.: Giving USA Foundation, 2008.

Collins, Mary Ellen. "Enjoy the Ride! How to Effectively Raise Funds in a Roller-Coaster Economy." *Advancing Philanthropy,* Feb. 2008.

"The Conference Board Consumer Confidence Index Plummets to an All-Time Low." New York: Conference Board, Oct. 28, 2008.

Court, David. "The Downturn's New Rules for Marketers." *McKinsey Quarterly,* Dec. 2008.

Craver, Roger. "Latest Fundraising Stats: Read 'Em and Weep!" *Agitator*, Sept. 30, 2008.

Craver, Roger. "Contrarian Fundraiser's Tips for Recession Recovery." *Agitator*, Dec. 15, 2008.

Dann, Jeremy. "Aggressive Marketing for Recessionary Times." *Network for Good*, Oct. 17, 2008.

Dunleavey, M. P. "Tight Times Even Tighter for Charities." *New York Times*, Nov. 15, 2008.

"Economic Climate and Giving." *Marts and Lundy Minute #3*, Sept. 2008.

Elischer, Tony, "Recession: Watching Is Not an Option." Buckingham, U.K.: Think Consulting Solutions, Nov. 2008.

Emma. "Beat the Downturn with Stylish Emails: Ten Trends for Emails That Pop." *Network for Good*, Oct. 15, 2008.

"Essential Questions for Fundraising in Troubled Times." The Jossey-Bass Nonprofit Series, Dec. 2008.

Flannery, Helen, Harris, Rob, and Rhine, Carol. "Index of National Fundraising Performance: 2008 Second Calendar Quarter Results." Charleston, S.C.: Target Analytics, Sept. 2008.

Friends of PRBO. "2008 Year-End Direct Mail Appeal." San Francisco: PRBO Conservation Science.

Fritz, Joanne. "Seven Fundraising Tips to Help Nonprofits Weather the Recession." About.com.

Fundraising Coach. "Tips for Fundraising in a Recession." Dec. 4, 2008.

"Fundraising Opportunities in a Changing Economic Climate." Charlotte, N.C.: Graham-Pelton Consulting, Nov. 2008.

Gilbert, Michael C. "Turning to Each Other in Hard Times: Four Steps for Saving Money and Building Social Capital." *Nonprofit Online News*, Nov. 25, 2008.

"Giving During Recessions and Economic Slowdowns." *Giving USA Spotlight*, no. 3, 2008.

Glier, John. "Philanthropy and the Economy." Chicago: Grenzebach, Glier and Associates, Oct. 30, 2008.

Gose, Ben. "Endowment Managers Consider How to Handle Downturn." *Chronicle of Philanthropy*, Oct. 2, 2008.

Hall, Holly. "Fund-Raising Strategies for Troubled Times." *Chronicle of Philanthropy*, Feb. 7, 2008.

Hall, Holly. "How Bad Is It?" *Chronicle of Philanthropy*, Oct. 2, 2008.

Hall, Holly. "Economy and Election Raise Specter of Depression-Era Fundraising." *Chronicle of Philanthropy*, Nov. 5, 2008.

Hall, Holly, and Wasley, Paula. "Holiday-Giving Update: Social-Services Groups See a Surge, But Most Groups Face Big Slowdown in Donations." *Chronicle of Philanthropy*, Dec. 15, 2008.

Head, George L. "Sustaining Nonprofits During Economic Downturns." Leesburg, Va.: Nonprofit Risk Management Center, n.d.

Hrywna, Mark. "Wall Street Meltdown Will Hit Charities When Cash Is Most Needed." *NonProfit Times*, Oct. 15, 2008.

Hurley, Tom. "Note to Public Broadcasting Clients." *DMW Direct*, Oct. 30, 2008.

Ibarra, Gonzalo. "10 medidas para tomar en tiempos turbulentos." Gonzaloibarra.com, Dec. 16, 2008.

Ideker, Paul. "Surviving Hard Times: A Guide for Cultural Organizations." *Arts Insights*, Oct. 2008.

"Integrating Online and Offline Campaigns." Big Duck and Convio, Nov. 2008.

Kibble, Kevin. "Recession-Proof Your Fundraising." *Global Connections*. London: Resource Alliance, 2008.

Krugman, Paul. "The Lame-Duck Economy." *New York Times*, Nov. 21, 2008.

Lagasse, Paul. "The Shifting Bottom Line." *Advancing Philanthropy*, Feb. 2008.

Lampman, Jane. "Despite Rough Economy, Americans Still Planning to Donate This Year." *ABC News*, Nov. 2, 2008.

Lautman, Maska, Neill & Company. "Smart Testing in Challenging Times." *DM News and Views*, Winter 2008.

Lawrence, Steven. "Do Foundation Giving Priorities Change in Times of Economic Distress?" *Foundation Center Research Advisory*, Nov. 2008.

Lees, Nelson. "Philanthropy Through Downturns: How the Giving Continues." Marts & Lundy Special Report, n.d.

McCoy, Kevin, and Dorell, Oren. "It's a Hard Time to Be a Charity." *USA Today*, Oct. 28, 2008.

"New Chart: Marketers Tailoring Digital Tactics in Recessionary Economy." Warren, R.I.: MarketingSherpa, Nov. 18, 2008.

Nonprofit Finance Fund. "Finance Questions to Consider: A Self-Assessment." New York: Nonprofit Finance Fund, n.d.

Nonprofit Finance Fund. "Navigating the Financial Crisis: Tips for Nonprofits." New York: Nonprofit Finance Fund, n.d.

O'Brien, Erica. "Direct Mail Is Not Dead." *Agitator*, Dec. 16, 2008.

Ogilvy, David. *Ogilvy on Advertising*. New York: Vintage Books, 1985.

Perry, Gail. "Successful Fundraising in Tough Times." *Philanthropy Journal*, Nov. 9, 2008.

Peters, Geoffrey W. "Fundraising in Difficult Times." Bowie, Md.: CDR Fundraising Group, Dec. 2008.

"Philanthropy in Uncertain Times: A Retrospective, 1931–1949." Memphis, Tenn.: Robert F. Sharpe & Co., 1991.

PricewaterhouseCoopers. UK Institute of Fundraising, Charity Finance Directors Group. "Managing in a Downturn: November 2008 Survey Results, Analysis and Key Messages." Dec. 1, 2008.

Raymond, Susan. "Hang on for the Ride? Not Enough." *OnPhilanthropy.* New York: Changing Our World, Oct. 1, 2008.

Rooney, Patrick M. "Giving and the Recession." *NPT Instant Fundraising*, Dec. 8, 2008.

Sauvé-Rodd, John. "The Recession and Its Effects on Fundraising." Talk delivered to direct marketing charity managers at the National Society for the Prevention of Cruelty to Children, London, Nov. 6, 2008.

Schwartz, Peter. *The Art of the Long View: Planning for the Future in an Uncertain World.* New York: Currency Doubleday, 1991.

Searle, Bob, and Neuhoff, Alex. "In Bad Economic Times, Focus on Impact." *Chronicle of Philanthropy*, Oct. 30, 2008.

"Seventh Annual GuideStar Nonprofit Economic Survey Reveals Significant Challenges for Charities." GuideStar, Oct. 29, 2008.

Sharpe Jr., Robert F. "Fundraising in Times of Uncertainty." Memphis, Tenn.: Sharpe Group, Oct. 20, 2008.

Sharpe Jr., Robert F. "Take It to the Next Level." *Trusts and Estates*, Sept. 2008.

Sharpe Jr., Robert F. "Where Do We Go from Here?" *Give and Take*, Nov. 2008.

Sheppard, Jim. "Secrets to Strong Giving in a Struggling Economy." Oct. 6, 2008. http://www.churchsolutionsmag.com/.

Strom, Stephanie. "Bracing for Lean Times Ahead." *New York Times*, Nov. 11, 2008.

"$3 Billion Is a Click Away." Convio, Online Fundraising Playbook Series, Oct. 2008.

"Tips for Fundraising in a Recession." *Fundraising Coach*, Dec. 4, 2008.

"Tips for Weathering the Economic Storm." *Marts and Lundy Philanthropy News*, Nov. 2008.

Triner, Sean. "Ten Steps to Managing Fundraising in a Recession." Sydney, Australia: Pareto Fundraising, 2008.

Voigt, Bradford W. "Resilient Philanthropy: How Various Economic Scenarios Affect Giving in the United States." *Advancing Philanthropy*, Oct. 2008.

Warwick, Mal. "Eight Ways Your Organization Can Cope with the Recession." *Opportunity Knocks*, 2008.

Warwick, Mal. *Testing, Testing, 1, 2, 3*. San Francisco: Jossey-Bass, 2003.

Warwick, Mal. *Revolution in the Mailbox, Revised Edition.* San Francisco: Jossey-Bass, 2004.

Warwick, Mal. *The Mercifully Brief, Real-World Guide to Raising $1,000 Gifts by Mail.* Medfield, Mass.: Emerson and Church, 2005.

Warwick, Mal, and Doyle, Dan. "Fundraising in Tough Economic Times." Berkeley, Calif.: Mal Warwick Associates, Jan. 2008.

Washington Regional Association of Grantmakers. "How Is the Economy Affecting Philanthropy in Our Region?" Washington, D.C.: Washington Regional Association of Grantmakers, Nov. 2008.

"What Boosts Lead Scores Now: Seven Tips for Surviving an Economic Downturn." Warren, R.I.: MarketingSherpa, Nov. 5, 2008.

"Why Fundraising May Flourish While Business Flounders." *Canadian Fundraiser eNews*, Dec. 15, 2008.

INDEX

the Road Again, 28, 31–32, 50; overview, 27–28; table of approaches and, 50

Economy: best practices for tight, 189–197; effect of downturns on nonprofits, 14–15; factoring in scenario planning, 23; historical perspectives of, 5–7; markers for correlating fundraising with, 7; name recognition in difficult, 36. *See also* Depressions; Economic recovery scenarios; Recessions

E-mail: chaperoned, 177–178; collecting addresses, 169, 170, 172; contacting supporters via, 171; fundraising by, 169; integrating with other approaches, 185–186; thank-you's via, 170

Emotional motivation, 80

Envelopes: colors of, 87–88; inserting pieces in, 117; plain vs. creative, 98–99; types of, 116

F

File maintenance, 106

Foundation grants, 9

Frequency of donations, 121, 122–123

Front-end premiums, 109–110

Fundraising: applying Boston matrix to, 66–73; assessing need for integrated campaigns, 179–181; best practices summarized, 189–197; costs of online, 113–114; delaying requests, 84; economic markers for correlating, 7; effectiveness of front-end premiums, 109–110; exploiting multiple channels for, 184; finding significant testing factors, 87–91; integrating approach to, 185–187, 196–197; making case

for giving, 79–80; making sure projects make money, 103–104; reassessing, 190; sticking with what works, 86–87; triggering donor responses to, 80–84; using high-priority testing for, 86, 87. *See also* Case for giving; Direct mail; Fundraising strategies

Fundraising strategies: aggressive approach, 45–47, 53–54; defensive approach, 39–41, 51–53; selective approach, 41–45; table of approaches and scenarios, 50

G

Gang-printing communications, 110–111

Gathering information, 22, 26

Gifts: communicating use and benefits of, 81; direct marketing for larger, 104–105; donor giving patterns, 182–184; during Great Depression, 15, 16; expressing benefits to donors, 81; giving levels, 121, 123–124; legacy, 33–34, 182–183; making Web contributions easy, 170, 171; outsourcing processing of, 106; phoning after receiving first, 139–140; recessions and corporate, 10; thanking donors for, 132–133, 135

Google Grants, 114, 173–174, 176

Grants: foundation, 9; Google Grants, 114, 173–174, 176

Great Depression, 12–15

Great Nonprofits, 175–176

Greenpeace, 196

GuideStar, 168

H

Happy Days Are Here Again recovery scenario: Aggressive

approach with, 54; future effects with, 28–30; overview, 27; Selective approach in, 55; winning strategy for, 50

High-dollar donors: direct mail responses and, 105; finding, 122–127, 192–193; rethinking small vs., 104–105

Human Rights Campaign, 196

I

Information silos. *See* Silo fundraising

Institutions. *See* Nonprofit organizations

Integrated fundraising campaigns: assessing need for, 179–181; reasons for, 181–184; suggestions for, 185–187

International nonprofit organizations, 37

J

Jones, John Price, 12, 14

L

Lapsed donors: phoning, 140; reactivating, 108–109

Legacy gifts, 33–34, 43, 182–183

M

Magazines, 105–106

Mailing lists: cleaning, 111–112; collecting e-mail addresses, 169, 170, 172; criteria for segmenting, 120–122; exchanging, 107–108; increasing with chaperoned e-mails, 177–178; locating high-dollar donors from, 120–129; segmenting, 119–120; testing, 90

Major gift officers: calling all donors, 138–139; measuring

effectiveness of, 103–104; rethinking differences in donors, 104–105

Mal Warwick Associates, 89

Marketing: applying Boston matrix to, 66–73; evaluating with Ansoff's matrix, 66, 73; incorporating case for giving in, 78; inexpensive donor research ideas, 140–141, 142–146; securing gifts of $1,000 with direct, 104–105. *See also* Direct mail

Maslow, Abraham, 80

Mechanical artwork, 118

Members: acquisition of, 43; surveys of, 143–144, 145–146. *See also* Donors

Mercifully Brief, Real-World Guide to Raising $1,000 Gifts by Mail (Warwick), 105

Midrange donors, 183–184, 187

Misery Loves Company recovery scenario: Aggressive approach with, 53; consequences of Defensive approach with, 51; future effects with, 32–35; overview, 28; Selective approach in, 54–55; winning strategy for, 50

Mission statements: describing how donations fulfill, 81; including in case for giving, 79, 84

Motivation: strengthening donor's, 75–77, 190–191; types of, 80

MoveOn.org, 177

Multiple fundraising channels, 184

N

Name recognition, 36

Newsletters, 105–106, 135, 170

Nonprofit organizations: basing decisions on results, 187–188; bonding donors with, 131, 134–136,